# THEOPHRASTUS
# DE VENTIS

# THEOPHRASTUS DE VENTIS

EDITED WITH INTRODUCTION,
TRANSLATION AND COMMENTARY

BY

## VICTOR COUTANT

Professor of Foreign Languages
Western Michigan University

AND

## VAL L. EICHENLAUB

Professor of Geography
Western Michigan University

UNIVERSITY OF NOTRE DAME PRESS
NOTRE DAME                                    LONDON

Library of Congress Cataloging in Publication Data

Theophrastus.
    De ventis.

    Greek text with English translation of Peri anemon
on opposite pages.
    Includes bibliographical references and index.
    1.  Winds--Early works to 1800.  2.  Winds--Levant--
Early works to 1800.  3.  Meteorology--History--Sources.
I.  Coutant, Victor Carlisle Barr, 1907-     II.  Eich-
enlaub, Val L., 1933-     III.  Title.
QC931.T4813     551.5'18     75-17766
ISBN 0-268-01829-4

# CONTENTS

# FOREWORD

A new English version of the <u>De Ventis</u> together
with discussions of the meteorological data and theories
of Theophrastus and with a textual apparatus should serve
several kinds of readers.  Students of long-term climatological trends will wish to have a reliable picture of
the weather around 300 B.C. in the eastern Mediterranean.
Students of the history of science will benefit by a
study of wind and weather theory, together with observations of surprising fineness and accuracy.  Students of
the history of philosophy will be interested in implications for both the shift in interests of the Peripatos
and for the degree of scholarly independence in that
school.  Students of classical antiquities will be at
least somewhat interested in the weather in Athens and
in a few other places in Greece as revealed in Theophrastus' short treatise.

# ACKNOWLEDGMENTS

We wish to acknowledge our appreciation to the following persons and agencies: the Faculty Research Fund of Western Michigan University for a research grant, which supported a part of the study; the staff of the Atmospheric Sciences Library, Silver Spring, Maryland, for their assistance in the research; the staff of the National Climatic Center, Asheville, North Carolina, for their assistance in a part of the research; James Wilson and Christina Bacon, for drawing maps and diagrams; Mrs. Charles Munk and Mrs. Monica Snyder, for the make-up and typing of the book; the administration of Western Michigan University for granting a sabbatical leave to pursue research; the staffs of the European libraries for assistance in using books and manuscripts of the Greek text; the Department of Geography for support in printing this book.

# INTRODUCTION

## I. The Greek Text

The text of the De Ventis was set down by Theophrastus at about 300 B.C. In Section 5 a reference is
made to a work on waters.[1] Seneca in Quaestiones Nat-
urales 3, 11, 3 speaks of finding in the De Aquis of
Theophrastus a description of the blockading of the
Gauls by Cassander in 310 B.C. and in Section 5 of the
De Ventis Theophrastus mentions the De Aquis as a work
already written. Thus the approximate dating is after
310 B.C.[2] The form of the treatise is that of lecture
notes, with the presumption of expansion during discussion and of opportunities for students to put questions.[3]
Like many works of Aristotle, it is fitted into the whole
corpus of the early Peripatetics through references to
other works of Aristotle and of Theophrastus himself,
through statements of purpose at the outset, or through
indications of the need or the intention to investigate
special topics more in detail.[4] The broad purpose of
the De Ventis, as with other works of Theophrastus, is
to replace or supplement the earlier works of Aristotle
because of new information gathered over a quarter of a
century or more and because of a change of view by Theophrastus.[5]

---

[1]Listed in Diogenes Laertius V 45.

[2]Peter Steinmetz, Die Physik des Theophrast von
Eresos, Gehlen, Bad Homburg, 1964, p. 28.

[3]Steinmetz, pp. 14-25.

[4]De Ventis passim, but especially Sec. 1, p. 4;
Meteorologica III, end.

[5]Steinmetz, pp. 115; 159ss; 325; Victor Coutant,
Theophrastus De Igne, Van Gorcum, Assen, 1971, Sec. 3.

Theophrastus conceives the universe as an integrated structure whose operations are based on scientific uniformitarianism.[6] Thus he can attack the etiology of atmospheric phenomena by putting them into a larger context, making them thus accessible to analytic and experimental processes. Parallelism and analogy are important.[7] The methodological basis for an experimental physics seems to be laid down; the hopes will be aborted. A very frequent procedure of Theophrastus in his exposition, like that of Aristotle, is to survey the possibilities of solutions to a question, including those offered by earlier thinkers, criticize them, and attempt either to draw the correct solution from among the choices or present a new view.[8]

Theophrastus uses for his sources, aside from Aristotle, materials gathered through trained colleagues and pupils from around the Mediterranean, the Lyceum being cosmopolitan in its membership (Heraclides Ponticus!), materials already available from Presocratics, and consultation with experienced personnel such as sailors and farmers. In the explanation of his findings he does not force his conclusions but leaves openings for further study. He performs modest experiments and analogizes from them to phenomena not susceptible of experimentation. He uses teleology only in the sense of the best and surest examples of a species or process.[9]

Certain aspects of Theophrastus' approach to the

---

[6]Ewald Wagner, "Der Syrische Auszug der Meteorologie des Theophrast" in Akademie der Wissenschaften und der Literatur, Mainz, Abhandlungen der Geistes und Sozialwissenschaftlichen Klassen, 1964, pp. 5-58.

[7]Wagner, p. 12.

[8]Wagner, p. 14.

[9]Steinmetz, pp. 322-324.

study of the cosmos should be mentioned: he does not hes-
itate to depart from doctrines of Aristotle; he tries to
do justice to detail while remaining systematic; he
emphasizes detailed facts and tends to avoid speculation;
he employs a pluralistic causation but rather as alter-
natives than as complementary factors.  In his physics
he adheres to a uniform physical system; he emphasizes
the hot, active element versus the three passive ele-
ments; he puts the sun in the center of activity as the
heat par excellence; the dry exhalation has lost much of
its role as an active force; he makes the chief operations of heat and cold those of:  (1) antiperistasis, the
concentration and recoil of heat by cold or simultaneous
mutual local replacement, (2) gravity and pressure, as
in the shift of the winds, (3) horror vacui, and in conjunction, antapodosis, the reciprocal exchange of matter,
the to-and-fro of the wind, for example; the extension
of the concept of hydrological flow to the winds.[10]

Material from Theophrastus' meteorology was used
by Epicurus,[11] Posidonius of Rhodes,[12] and Seneca,[13]
among other ancients, and later by Syrian and Arabic
writers.  We have included in our Commentary passages
from the latter group, translated from Reitzenstein's
German into English, where parallel passages exist.[14]

---

[10]Steinmetz, pp. 324-328.

[11]E. Reitzenstein, "Theophrast bei Epikur und
Lukrez," Orient und Antike 2, 1924, Heidelberg, pp. 5-106.

[12]Steinmetz, p. 8, note 11.

[13]Steinmetz, pp. 68-73.

[14]From the editions of Bergsträsser, Wagner, and
Reitzenstein (see bibliography).

## Manuscripts of the <u>De Ventis</u>

D   Vossianus Graecus Q 25, Late 15th century, Univer-
siteitsbibliotheek, Leiden.

E   Neapolitanus Graecus III D 1, 1497, Biblioteca
Nazionale, Naples.

I   Palatinus Graecus 162, 1442-1457, Bibliotheca Vaticana, Rome.

L   Reginensis Graecus 123, ca. 1500, Bibliotheca Vaticana, Rome.

M   Urbinas Graecus 108, Early 15th century, Bibliotheca
Vaticana, Rome.

O   Vaticanus Graecus 1305, Late 15th century, Bibliotheca Vaticana, Rome.

P   Vaticanus Graecus 1302, 13th century, Bibliotheca
Vaticana, Rome.

Q   Ambrosianus Graecus P. 80 Sup., Early 15th century,
Bibliotheca Ambrosiana, Milan.

R   Marcianus Graecus 260, 1442-1459, Biblioteca Nazionale Marciana, Venice.

U   Parisinus Graecus 2277, Late 15th century, Bibli-
othèque Nationale, Paris.

X   Bongarsius Graecus 402, 1480-1500, Bürgerbibliothek,
Bern.

Z   Londiniensis Graecus, Add. 5113, Late 15th century,
British Museum, London.

Latin Version - Parisinus Latinus 11,857 by J. Dale-
campius.

In view of the accomplishment of Walter Burnikel
in his <u>Textgeschichtliche</u> <u>Untersuchungen</u> <u>zu</u> <u>Neun</u> <u>Opuscula</u>
<u>Theophrasts</u>, Steiner, Wiesbaden, 1974, through wide-rang-
ing and penetrating study of all related manuscripts in
achieving a stemma, it is unnecessary to do more than
indicate the stemma for the <u>De Ventis</u> by modifying that
which he prints on Page 90 of his work. In reading the
report of his investigations we are confident that his
results will withstand close inspection and that previous efforts in the <u>De Igne</u> and the <u>De Lapidibus</u>[15] fall

---

[15]Coutant's edition of the <u>De Igne</u> and D. E.

either short of or wide of the mark.

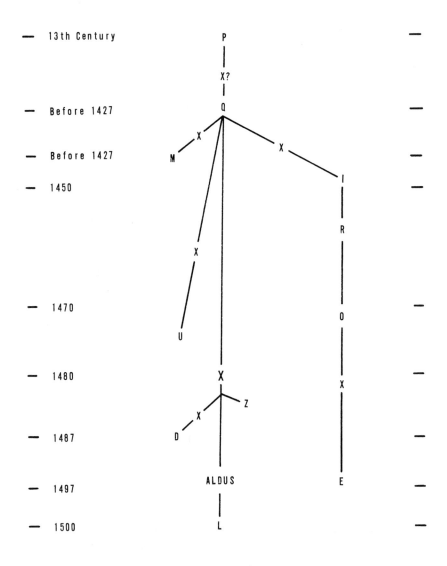

— 13th Century
— Before 1427
— Before 1427
— 1450
— 1470
— 1480
— 1487
— 1497
— 1500

Eichholz' edition of the <u>De Lapidibus</u>, Clarendon, Oxford,
1965, pp. 141.

Editions and Commentaries

| | |
|---|---|
| Aldus | Aristoteles et Theophrastus, Vol. II, Venice, 1497. |
| Oporinus, J. | Basel, 1541. Hardly more than a reprint of Aldus. |
| Turnebus | Greek text of unknown date, not seen by us and reported from Bonaventura and Schneider in good faith. |
| Turnebus | Latin Translation in Schneider, Vol. II. |
| Vascosanus | Greek text, Paris, 1551. |
| Margo Vascosani | The same, with marginal notes by an unknown hand, in the Universiteits-bibliotheek, Leiden. |
| Camotius, J. B. | Venice, 1552. Not greatly different from Aldus. |
| Bonaventura, F. (A) | Theophrasti De Ventis Liber, Urbino, 1593. Latin translation. |
| Bonaventura, F. (B) | De Causa Ventorum Motus, Urbino, 1592. On ancient theory. |
| Bonaventura, F. (C) | Adnotationes in Librum Theophrasti De Ventis, Venice, 1593. |
| Furlanus, D. | Theophrasti Eresii...Pleraque, Hanau, 1605, Text, translation, notes. |
| Heinsius, D. | Theophrasti Eresii...Opera Omnia, Leiden, 1613. Text and translation. |
| Salmasius, C. | Exercitationes Plinianae, Paris, 1629. Notes. |
| Schneider, J. G. | Theophrasti Opera Omnia, Leipzig, 1818-1822. Includes emendations proposed by Adamantios Coray in Vol. V, pp. 159-163 and by others in IV, pp. 680-719. Text, Latin translation, commentary. |
| Wimmer, F. | Opera Omnia, Breslau, 1842; Leipzig, 1854; Paris, 1866. Text. (Latin translation in last only). |
| Wood, J. G. and G. J. Symonds | Theophrastus on Winds and Weather Signs, No Text; translation, introduction, notes. Stanford, London, 1894. |

Works Related to the <u>De Ventis</u> and to Meteorology

Bergsträsser, G.     <u>Neue Meteorologische Fragmente des</u>
<u>Theophrast</u>--Sitzungsberichte d.
Heidelberger Akademie d. Wissenschaften, Phil.-Hist. Klasse,
1918, 9.

Böker, R.     "Winde"--<u>Pauly-Wissowa Real-Enzyklo-</u>
<u>padie</u> VIII A2 (1958) 2211ss.

Burnikel, W.     <u>Textgeschichtliche Untersuchungen</u>
<u>zu Neun Opuscula Theophrasts,</u>
Steiner, Wiesbaden, 1974.

Coutant, V.     <u>Theophrastus De Igne</u>, Van Gorcum,
Assen, 1971.

Drossaart-     The Syriac Translation of Theophras-
Lulofs, H. J.     tus' Meteorology--<u>Autour d'Aristote</u>,
<u>Recueil d'Etudes</u> etc. <u>offert a Mgr.</u>
<u>A. Mansion</u>, Publications Universi-
taires, Louvain, 1955, pp. 443-449.

Eichholz, D.     <u>Theophrastus De Lapidibus</u>, Clarendon, Oxford, 1965.

Flashar, H.     <u>Aristoteles, Problemata Physica,</u>
Akademie, Berlin, 1962.

Gilbert, O.     <u>Die Meteorologischen Theorien des</u>
<u>Griechischen Altertums</u>, Olms, Hilde-
sheim, 1967 (reprinted).

Regenbogen, O.     "Theophrastos von Eresos"--<u>Pauly-</u>
<u>Wissowa Real-Enzyklopädie</u>, Supple-
ment-band 7, 1354ss.

Reitzenstein, E.     "Theophrast bei Epikur und Lukrez,"
<u>Orient</u> und <u>Antike</u> 2, 1924, Heidel-
berg, pp. 5-106.

Solmsen, F.     <u>Aristotle's System of the Physical</u>
<u>World</u>, Cornell University Press,
Ithaca, 1960.

Stange, A.     <u>Versuch einer Darstellung der</u>
<u>Griechischen Windverhältnisse</u> und
<u>ihrer Wirkungsweise</u>, C. E. Klin-
kicht, Meissen, 1910.

Steinmetz, P.     <u>Die Physik des Theophrast von</u>
<u>Eresos</u>, Gehlen, Bad Homburg, 1964.

Strohm, H. (A)     "Untersuchungen zur Entwicklungs-
geschichte d. aristotelischen
Meteorologie"--<u>Philologus</u>, 1935
Supplementband 28, #1, pp. 1-28.

Strohm, H. (B)          "Zur Meteorologie des Theophrast"--
                        Philologus 92, 1937, 249-268; 401-
                        428.

Wagner, Ewald           "Der syrische Auszug der Meteorol-
                        ogie des Theophrast"--Akademie der
                        Wissenschaften und der Literatur,
                        Mainz, Abhandlungen der Geistes-
                        und Sozialwissenschaftlichen
                        Klassen, 1964, 5-58.

Related Ancient Texts

Aristotle               Meteorologica, edited by H. D. P.
                        Lee, Heinemann, London, 1962.

Aristotle               Problems, edited by W. S. Hett,
                        Heinemann, London, 1961-1965.

Theophrastus            Enquiry into Plants, Vol. II,
                        edited by A. Hort, Heinemann, Lon-
                        don, 1916 ("Concerning Weather
                        Signs").

It should be noted that the treatise on weather
signs is later than Theophrastus but contains some material from his works; the Problems were compiled later
than Aristotle and contain material from many sources.
Those concerning winds come mainly from the De Ventis,
but not all, and in some cases the reverse is true.

## II. The Observations of Theophrastus
## Regarding Winds

Observations on the behavior of the winds abound throughout the treatise, in line with the detailed and empirical nature of the work. Many of the observations were undoubtedly relayed to Theophrastus by travellers, colleagues, and myths, although some were probably observed directly by him in his travels. It seems certain that carefully kept wind data were also accessible to him. Böker[16] believes that there was a weather station on Cape Sigeum (near Troy), whose observations and terminology played an important role in ancient navigation, and that the larger harbor towns had manuals of navigation which supplied wind information.

In attesting to the accuracy of Theophrastus' numerous observational statements, we are handicapped by the fact that available modern data are not ipso facto representative of wind conditions during Theophrastus' time. Until recently the concept of climatic constancy has colored historical investigation, probably as an over-reaction to early 20th century environmental determinism. Significant changes in climate occurring during the historical period have now been substantiated.[17]

The transitional location of Greece and the Mediterranean, between two major wind belts, conditions the area to be sharply responsive to the contractions or expansions of the global wind belts which may accompany climatic fluctuations. Consequently, if the climate dur-

---

[16]R. Böker, "Winde," Pauly-Wissowa Real-Enzyklopädie, VIII A2, 1958, 2264.

[17]H. H. Lamb, "The New Look of Climatology" Nature, Vol. 223, 1969, pp. 1209-1214. The dynamic nature of climate and the rather startling magnitude of past climate change during historical times have been examined in new perspective in this article.

ing Theophrastus' day differed substantially from that of the present, his observations regarding the winds would be pertinent to a contrasting meteorological and climatic regime, for which we have no verifying data. Should the modern data substantiate his statements, meaningful evidence may, in turn, be provided that the wind systems of the classical period did not differ greatly from those of the 20th century.

Interest in climatic change in Ancient Greece was stimulated in 1966 by the work of the classical archeologist Rhys Carpenter.[18] Carpenter presented the thesis that discontinuities in Greek civilization (arrival of Dorians in 1000 B.C. and of Slavs in 700 A.D.) were instigated by rather abrupt climatic changes involving drought patterns which caused famine and depopulation. Carpenter's ideas, although controversial and not directly related to the question of climate during Theophrastus' day, alerted paleoclimatologists to the large gap in climatic information from the classical Greek period. In a review of Carpenter's work, the eminent British climatologist H. H. Lamb pointed out that although knowledge of climatic change in the middle and northern latitudes of Europe has been fairly well substantiated from pollen analysis of numerous bog and lake site deposits, "by comparison, the Mediterranean is a strangely neglected region despite the many ancient cultures there and the wealth of literature which has survived."[19]

---

[18]Rhys Carpenter, Discontinuity in Greek Civilization (The J. H. Gray Lectures for 1965) Cambridge: University Press, 1966. 88 pp.

[19]H. H. Lamb, "Climatic Changes during the Course of Early Greek History" Antiquity, Vol. 42, 1968, p. 232.

A.  The Winds of Greece and the Aegean During the Present Era

The prevailing winds of Greece and the Aegean are a response to controls exerted by atmospheric pressure systems in their average and seasonal positions, and to more localized factors, including topography, coastal configuration, and insular location. The atmospheric controls are normally dominant, but at times, and in certain locales, the geographic controls completely overshadow the larger-scale atmospheric features as causative factors.

Atmospheric Controls:  Greece has a characteristic Mediterranean climate, which, although rather famous, actually is not widespread, occupying only about 1.7% of the earth's land area.[20] The Mediterranean climate is characterized by rainy, mild winters and dry, warm-to-hot summers. Typically, areas which enjoy a Mediterranean type of climate are located transitionally between the belt of westerlies of the middle latitudes, with its abundant cyclonic activity and substantial variability of winds, and the dry subsiding air of the subtropics, associated with the subtropical high pressure cell. During the winter the westerlies, with their numerous cyclonic depressions and frequent rain-giving episodes, control the weather. During the summer, the characteristic uniformity of the subtropics, with aridity and almost cloudless skies, dominates for long periods of time.

In winter, Greece and the Aegean are controlled by a maximum of barometric pressure over Asia, with a tongue

---

[20]Glenn T. Trewartha, An Introduction to Climate, 4th ed., McGraw-Hill, New York, 1968, p. 281.

which advances westward over eastern Europe.[21] Air which
is cold and dry, and of continental origin, flows from
this pressure maximum to give the area prevailing northerly winds during the cooler months of the year. At the
same time, however, the Mediterranean is a region of
lower pressure, located between the Atlantic pressure
maximum (subtropical high) and the eastern European pressure maximum. Consequently it is frequently traversed by
cyclonic depressions with their counterclockwise and con-
vergent wind fields. Thus, when the area is affected by
these disturbances, winds may become highly variable,
shifting in a clockwise direction (veering) if the disturbance passes to the north, and in a counterclockwise
direction (backing) if the disturbance passes to the
south. As a result of the large frequency of cyclonic
depressions during the winter, and also in spring and
fall, winds are more variable during the cold season,
although the northerly winds tend to be most frequent.

In the summer, a much more stable weather pattern
prevails. Cyclonic depressions are practically non-ex-
istent in the Mediterranean, and winds become more regular than during the winter. The tongue of high pressure in eastern Europe disappears, and a strong minimum
of barometric pressure develops over northwestern India
and Pakistan. At the same time, the subtropical high
over the Atlantic shifts northward, creating a rather
marked west to east pressure gradient over the Mediterranean. During this time of the year, northerly winds
blow over the Aegean with a great frequency. These winds
were called by the ancients "etesians" (yearly) and col-

---

[21]E. G. Mariolopoulos, An Outline of the Climate
of Greece, Publications of the Meteorological Institute
of the University of Athens, #6, Athens, 1961, p. 41.

loquially, today, are called "meltemi."[22] The etesians occur between May and October, obtaining greatest frequency in July and August. In May, when they are usually weak and unsteady, they were referred to as "prodromoi" (precursors) or forerunners by the ancients.

Thus the atmospheric controls determine that prevailing winds will be from the north, with great steadiness during the summer period of etesians, but also, although with less persistence, during the winter. The much more unstable winter weather regime gives rise also to some characteristic winds. The "scirocco" is a warm south or southwest wind which may blow from November until May. It is related to the passage of cyclonic depressions across the Mediterranean. In Africa it is usually a warm, dry wind, but in passage across the Mediterranean it acquires considerable moisture and may bring rain to the northern shores. Winds called "ornithiai" (bird winds) by the ancient Greeks may also occur, generally in the spring. They are cold north or northeast winds, which may be accompanied by snow and abnormally cold weather. Also in the spring occur south winds which bring clear weather, the "leuconotoi."

Local Winds: Superimposed on this general wind pattern are countless localized winds resulting from the vagaries of topography and the extensive, strongly indented coastline. Land and sea breezes are very common along the coasts of Greece and the Aegean, particularly during the warmer period of the year. They occur because of localized heating differences arising as a result of

---

[22]D. A. Metaxas, "A Contribution to the Study of the Etesian Winds" Presented at the Mediterranean Meteorological Conference, under the auspices of Navy Weather Research Facility, in Norfolk, Virginia, June 1970, p. 1.

the different heating rates of land and water surfaces.
Sea breezes usually spring up during the late morning or
early afternoon, blowing from the sea toward the land.
The land breeze occurs at night and is usually much less
noticeable, blowing from the land to the sea. Sea breezes
may be powerful enough to counteract the prevailing etesians, as is the case in the area of Athens, where the
sea breeze from the south or southwest blows during the
middle of the day in opposition to the prevailing northerly etesians.

Fallwinds are common in the mountainous terrain of
Greece, and along the coasts of some of the mountainous
islands of the Aegean. These are winds which descend
from higher elevations and undergo heating because of the
increased pressures to which they are subjected. Fallwinds can on occasion be desiccating to vegetation. The
"bora" is common, particularly along the Adriatic coastline during the winter. The bora results when accumula-
tions of cold air over the higher interior areas rush
outward, descending as a high velocity wind to the coastal areas. Boras are cold winds, as the heating by compression which the air currents undergo is not sufficient
to offset the marked contrast in temperature between the
cold interior and relatively warm coastal zones. Although
most common and forceful along the eastern Adriatic coastline, they may also occur throughout other portions of
Greece and the Aegean.

An array of mountain and valley winds is also in-
digenous to Greece. These winds occur in rough terrain
as a result of unequal surface heating. Mountain winds
blow down the valleys at night, while valley winds blow
upward along the valleys and their strongly heated slopes
during the day. In regions where the topography is conducive to their development, they may, like land and sea
breezes, become the dominant winds.

B.  The Wind Systems of Ancient Greece

Indirect evidence, for the most part, must be utilized in reconstructing the wind patterns existing in the
eastern Mediterranean in 300 B.C.  A number of investigators have examined the climatic patterns in northern and
central Europe in the several millenia preceding the
birth of Christ.  These hold certain implications for the
Aegean and eastern Mediterranean.  Brooks,[23] using evidence from peat bog studies, suggested that a sudden increase in rainfall and a cooling trend for Europe as a
whole occurred at about 500 B.C. with the climate of 0
A.D. about similar to the climate of 1949.  Frenzel,[24]
in reviewing botanical evidence, suggested that at some-
time between 900-700 B.C. the climate of Europe became
more oceanic with improved water balance and a decrease
in mean annual temperature.  Geomorphological evidence
suggested to Starkel[25] the following post glacial periods
in Europe:

| | |
|---|---|
| Pre-Boreal | 8300-7900 B.C. |
| Boreal | 7900-6200 B.C. |
| Atlantic | 6200-3000 B.C. |
| | (Climatic Optimum, signifi- |
| | cantly warmer than present) |
| Sub-Boreal | 3000-500 B.C. |
| | (Cooling) |
| Sub-Atlantic | 500 B.C. |
| | (Coolest) |

---

[23]C. E. P. Brooks, Climate Through the Ages,
McGraw-Hill, New York, 1949, P. 299.

[24]B. Frenzel "Climatic Change in the Atlantic/Sub-
Boreal Transition on the Northern Hemisphere," Proceed-
ings of the International Symposium on World Climate 8000
B.C. to ) A.D., J. S. Sawyer, (ed.), Royal Meteorological
Society, London, 1966, pp. 99-123.

[25]L. Starkel, "Post-glacial Climate and the Moulding of European Relief" Proceedings of the International

Starkel stated that marked cooling occurred early in the
Sub-Atlantic with frosty and snowy winters in Northern
Europe and heavy rainfall during cooler summers in that
area. Lamb[26] agrees in general with the basic climatic
regimes outlined above. He recognizes a decline in temperature from the Climatic Optimum (Atlantic period of
Starkel), and the onset in about 500 B.C. of a rainy,
cool period. Lamb states that no really dry season occurred in the Mediterranean area as exists today, and
that in classical Greece from 800 B.C. onwards there was
plenty of forest and more rainfall than today. In yet
another study,[27] Lamb quotes the Roman agricultural writers in 100 B.C. as noting that the vine and olive were
spreading north in Italy to districts where the weather
was formerly too severe--indicating that the trend had
reversed and previous centuries had cooler temperatures.

Thus, available evidence strongly suggests that
the wind patterns in Greece and the Aegean c. 300 B.C.
represent those which occurred during a period of declin-
ing temperature. Theophrastus comments on this cooling
trend which accompanied the Sub-Atlantic stage (Section
13) in referring to the large snowfall amounts on the
summits of Crete and failure of crops in areas which were
formerly productive. This deterioration of climate was
apparently well recognized by the Greeks, as was the in-
herent instability of climate in relation to food supply

Symposium on World Climate 8000 to 0 B.C., J. S. Sawyer,
(ed.), Royal Meteorological Society, London, 1966, pp.
15-23.

[26]H. H. Lamb, The Changing Climate, Methuen and
Co., London, 1966, p. 6.
[27]H. H. Lamb "On the Nature of Certain Climatic
Epochs Which Differed from the Modern (1900-1939) Nor-
mal" Changes of Climate, Proceedings of Rome Symposium,
UNESCO and WMO, 1963, pp. 125-149.

and settlement processes. Two questions may be raised:
(1) what were the prevailing wind patterns during this
period, and (2) what contrasts existed compared to the
present?

Charts of mean atmospheric pressures over the
northern hemisphere have been prepared for 6500 B.C.,
4000 B.C., 2000 B.C. and 500 B.C.[28] From these reconstructions the mean wind field can be derived at each
time interval. A comparison of these maps for 500 B.C.
with current mean pressure charts will give information
regarding circulation features at the onset of the Sub-
Atlantic period as compared to the present. From this
information an extrapolation may be made to 300 B.C. with
consideration of changes in the mean pressure and wind
fields which would exacerbate the cooling which was already in progress.

Both the climatic evidence and the reconstruction
of mean pressure patterns by Lamb et. al. suggest that
in 300 B.C. the prevailing wind patterns in Greece did
not depart widely from those of the present. The presence of a considerable extent of pack ice in the Arctic
is an important variable in the determination of atmospheric circulation patterns. Pack ice, which had re-
treated considerably or disappeared during the Atlantic
period (6200-3000 B.C.) had re-formed or readvanced prior
to Theophrastus' time, and reconstructions of winter and
summer pressure patterns by Lamb for 500 B.C. rather
closely resemble present conditions with the following
exceptions: (1) summer polar low, weaker and displaced
westward (2) winter subtropical high, ridged eastward

---

[28]H. H. Lamb, R. P. W. Lewis, and A. Woodroffe,
"Atmospheric Circulation and Main Climatic Variables
between 8000 B.C. and 0 B.C.: Meteorological Evidence,"
Proceedings of the International Symposium on World
Climate 8000 B.C. to 0 B.C., J. S. Sawyer, (ed.), Royal
Meteorological Society, London, pp. 174-217.

over the Mediterranean. Shifts of these anomalous features closer to present patterns could account for the cooler summers, frostier winters, greater rainfall, and increased marineness in Europe in the centuries subsequent to 500 B.C. as suggested by geomorphological and botanical evidence.

It seems reasonable to conclude that although the prevailing winds in Greece at 300 B.C. may not have been exactly similar to those of the present, it is unlikely that any marked contrasts existed. Fortunately then, an attempt to validate Theophrastus' observations by employing current data seems justifiable, and if his statements appear factual, the belief that the climate of classical Greece was similar to that of the present is reinforced.

C. Accuracy of Observation in De Ventis

Observations on the winds in De Ventis fall generally within five main categories: (1) observations on the seasonal frequencies and force of the winds, (2) observations concerning the nature of the etesians, (3) observations concerning local winds, (4) observations concerning the characteristics of the various individual winds, and (5) physiological effects of winds.

Observations concerning the seasonal frequencies and force of the wind: Both Aristotle and Theophrastus correctly note the dominance of north and south winds at Athens, and their forceful nature. Theophrastus states in Section 2: "The north winds and the south winds are strong winds and blow the longest time." In Section 10 he comments: "The north winds blow in winter, at the beginning of spring, and at the end of late autumn." The statement is highly accurate (Figure 1), particularly when one considers that the wind directions of the

Greeks were very specific, utilizing a windrose based on
solstitial sunrise and sunset. Data on wind velocities[29]
also confirm Theophrastus' statement that the north and
south winds blow with greater force than other winds.

The south winds of spring (leuconotoi) were
thought to arise at a definite time after the winter solstice,[30] and had been confused with the birdwinds (ornithiai) by Aristotle, whose rise he sets at the 70th
day after the winter solstice (Meteorologica 362a 22-33).
These, however, were moist northerly winds, which according to tradition blew in Greece for a series of days in
February and March at the time of bird migrations.

In Section 48, the variability of the west wind
is attested by the statement that it "blows in two seasons only, the spring and late autumn." The data (Figure 2) confirm the accuracy of the statement with peaks
of frequencies in April and June, and another peak in
the late autumn, although the west wind is not precluded
from blowing in other seasons. The afternoon periodicity of the west wind alluded to in Section 41 is also
confirmed by modern data, a further implication that the
Greeks must have been very careful wind observers and had
rather precise data available to them.

Observations concerning wind frequencies in Egypt
are less acute. In Section 5 Theophrastus states: "For
those who live in Egypt and nearby, the situation is reversed. The south wind has force." And in Section 6:
"Thus, down there the south wind is more frequent, uniform, continuous, and regular." In fact, wind data for

---

[29]Sources of data are listed in the bibliography.

[30]Böker, 2368. The leuconotoi are winds of fair
weather and almost cloud-free skies. They are change-
able in duration from year to year and are noticeable
only to a keen observer, but are much in contrast to the
usual dark, rainy south winds.

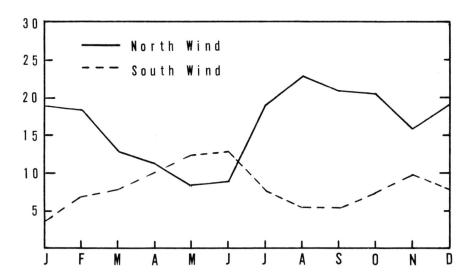

Figure 1. Surface winds at Athens, frequency in percent (from Data Processing Division, ETAC/USAF, Air Weather Service/MAC).

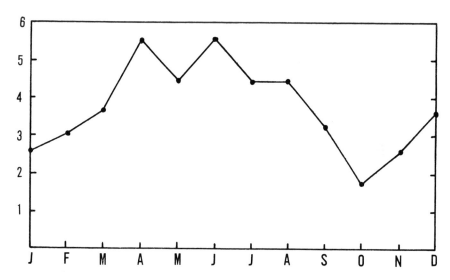

Figure 2. West winds at Athens, frequency in percent (from Data Processing Division, ETAC/USAF. Air Weather Service/MAC).

Egypt suggest just the opposite,[31] and Theophrastus appears to attempt to mesh facts to fit the concept of reciprocity, which is an integral part of his anemology.

Observations Concerning the Character of the Etesians: The characteristics of these persistent northerly or northeasterly winds during the summer months were well known to the ancient Greeks,[32] and De Ventis contains many accurate observations concerning these winds. Theophrastus recognizes that their intensity varied from year to year (Section 12), a fact confirmed by modern studies[33]. The marked diurnal variability[34] of these winds is noted in Section 11, as is the occurrence of "prodromoi" (forerunners) in June, before the onset of the etesians proper.

----

[31]Only in Lower Egypt do southerly winds occur with any frequency, and then primarily during the winter months. They occur in that area when depressions move across the Mediterranean to the north causing south and southwesterly winds along the immediate coast. Upper Egypt is practically unaffected by these depressions, remaining for the most part under the effects of the subtropical high pressure cell that covers the western desert of Egypt. Thus the prevailing winds throughout the year are northerly. (J. Griffiths, (ed.) Climates of Africa, Vol. 10 of World Survey of Climatology, Elsevier Publishing Co., New York, 1972, p. 91.

[32]Leon N. Carapiperis, The Etesian Winds, I. The Opinions of the Ancient Greeks on the Etesian Winds, Ethnikon Asterokospeion Hypomnemata Ser. II, Meteorologica, No. 9, Athens, 1962, 17pp.

[33]Leon N. Carapiperis, "On the Periodicity of the Etesians in Athens" Weather, Vol. VI, 1951, p. 378-379. Carapiperis found a positive correlation between the sunspot number and total number of days with etesians during the year.

[34]D. A. Metaxas, A Contribution to the Study of Etesian Winds, Presented at the Mediterranean Meteorological Conference, Norfolk, Virginia, June, 1970, 18 pp. The strong diurnal variability of the velocity of the Etesians is discussed.

In section 4, the tendency for the etesians to become more cloudy and develop rain showers as they flow southward across the Mediterranean is discussed.[35]

The cooling, beginning about 500 B.C., which accompanied the Sub-Atlantic stage in Europe was correctly linked by Theophrastus to possible changes in prevailing winds, as manifested by the summer etesians (Section 13).[36] However, the nature of the link was interwoven with Aristotelian concepts and myth. The etesians, according to Theophrastus and Aristotle, occurred as a result of melting of the snows of the north. During the earlier period, with warmer temperatures and less snowfall, the vigor of the etesians must have been diminished, Theophrastus reasons. Thus the myth is called into play:

> If the etesians ever failed (and Aristaeus recalled them, according to the myth, by sacrificing to Zeus on Ceos) the exposed territories were not subjected to rain and snow as now (Section 14).

The myth referred to is the old story that Sirius used to burn up the Cyclades, and the islands suffered from hunger and disease, until an appeal was made to Aristaeus, the son of Apollo and Cyrene.[37] Aristaeus went to Ceos to build an altar in honor of Zeus, master of rainfalls, and offered sacrifices to Sirius on the peaks of the high mountains. Zeus answered the appeal by sending the etesians on earth to blow and refresh the archipelago for forty days.

<u>Observations of Local Winds</u>: With much mountain-

---

[35]Moisture is acquired, and showers may occur along elevated coastlines.

[36]Metaxas, p. 14, discusses the relation of the etesians to prevailing upper air patterns, and hence to climatic change.

[37]Carapiperis, "The Opinions of the Ancient Greeks on the Etesian Winds," p. 2.

ous terrain and indented coastline, Greece and the Aegean have long been known for locally derived and orographically controlled wind systems. Many wind pecularities related to topography are noted in De Ventis. In Section 27, the "backlash" of winds (a counterflow, with southerly winds near the surface and prevailing northerly winds aloft) near Aegae in Macedonia is described. Aegae (now called Edhessa) lies south of the Bora Mountains and east of Begorritis Lake. There seems little doubt that Theophrastus is referring to a combination lake and valley wind, where the vegetation-bare south wall of the Bora favors formation of a southerly upslope wind in opposition to the prevailing etesians.[38]

The marked sea breeze from the south and southwest at Athens during the period of etesians made a strong impression on Theophrastus,[39] and in Section 28 he comments on the sea breezes on the south coast of Euboea, which have caught the attention of modern investigators.[40]

The presence of fallwinds and their rather spectacular effects elicit comments.[41] Some fallwinds are recognized by their desiccating characteristics, as the fallwinds of the Malic Gulf area and Pierian Gulf in Thessaly (Section 45). Others are puzzling to Theophrastus, as the fallwinds at Plataea, in Boetia, which lies on the north slope of Mt. Cithaeron, and may be subjected

---

[38]Böker, 2257.

[39]For a detailed account of sea breezes in the Athens area cf. Hannes An der Lan, "Meteorologische Besonderheiten der Ägäis" Archiv Fur Meteorologie, Geophysik und Bioclimatologie, Band I (1949), 288-409.

[40]An der Lan, p. 395.

[41]Probably the best discussion of fallwinds along the Greek coast is contained in An der Lan, Part II "Lokale Fallwinde im griechischen Küstengebiet" pp. 390-396.

to strong fallwinds when the southerly scirocco is blowing, but is relatively protected from northerly winds.

Characteristics of Individual Winds: The empirical nature of the treatise and emphasis on detailed
observation lead to numerous comments on the characteristics of individual winds. In Section 5, Theophrastus
cites a proverb which alludes to the tendency of the
south wind to increase in vigor, while the north wind is
more forceful at its inception, decreasing with time.
The statement is descriptive of wind systems surrounding
cyclones as they progress across the eastern Mediterranean. With a cyclone travelling a more northerly track,
south winds herald the approach of the depression center.
They gradually increase in velocity as the depression
approaches, reaching their maximum velocity prior to
frontal passage, when they cease to blow, being replaced
by winds from a northerly direction. These are most
forceful at their inception, gradually dying as the cyclone moves on to the east.
      In Section 6, the north wind is characterized as
being cloudy near its origin, but fair in places far from
its origin, while the reverse is true for the south wind,
an accurate observation concerning the tendency of winds
in the northern hemisphere to converge and increase in
cloudiness moving northward, diverge and decrease in
cloudiness moving southward. In Section 9, the north
wind is noted as quickly following the south wind, and
not the other way around, stemming from the tendency of
fallwinds and boras to occur suddenly on south-facing
shores of islands and coasts, and the quick wind changes
to northerly quadrants which follow cold front passages.
      The veering (clockwise) turning of winds with the
approach of a cyclone and subsequent passage north of
Greece is correctly perceived by Theophrastus (Section

52), as is the quick change of wind direction accompanying frontal passage.

Physiological Effects: Theophrastus recognizes that the various winds have a distinct effect on human response and behavior. In Section 56, the debilitating effects of humid, warm south winds are commented on. The warmth and humidity brought by the south wind was a common sensation to those residing in Greece and the Aegean, just as it is to the inhabitants of eastern North America. On the other hand, "...south winds when dry and not rainy produce fever" (Section 57). The north wind, as in eastern North America, is drier and more invigorating. The effects of the winds are also felt on crops and inanimate objects. With a moist south wind, gut strings break and glued joints crack (Section 58). Iron is also more easily prepared. On the other hand, the ironworkers are more vigorous when the north wind is blowing, as it is drier and more stimulating (Section 58).

D. Summary

The high degree of accuracy of Theophrastus' observations bespeak carefully kept data, accumulated over a substantial number of years. Intuition or subjective conclusions can be virtually ruled out as a basis of his factual statements. The majority of his observations concerning Greece and the Aegean are supported by modern data, a fact which in itself is further evidence that the climate of Theophrastus' time was not greatly different from that of the present.

Observations concerning the winds of foreign regions are much less accurate, indicating that Theophrastus relied more on hearsay, proverb, and myth for his knowledge of areas outside the Aegean. Additionally, he,

like Aristotle, occasionally fell victim to deductive
traps.  Illustrative are his statements concerning prevailing winds in Egypt.

A. Background

Evaluation of the Theophrastean anemology must
proceed from an appreciation of theories put forth by
Aristotle in the Meteorologica. It seems conclusive that
the Aristotelian concepts represented a departure from
the prevailing thoughts of the time as conceived by the
Presocratic philosophers, including Anaximander, Anaximenes, Empedocles, Democritus, and Heraclitus. Aristotle's
objections to previous meteorological theories were based
on the assumption of generation and destruction of earth,
air, fire, and water.[43] Failure to account for this in-
teraction was sufficient to invalidate all previous theories.

Central to the Aristotelian presentation were the
denial that wind was simply air in motion, and the etio-
logical innovation which springs from this refutation,
the doctrine of the double anathymiasis, the warm-dry and
cold-moist exhalations. Although a moist terrestrial exhalation seemed firmly fixed in Presocratic thought,
probably due to the observation of rising mist, the warm-
dry exhalation was the key to Aristotle's innovative system, representing the transformation from earth to fire.

In Meteorologica, 349a 8-22 Aristotle polemicised
against unnamed thinkers in his denial of wind as air in

---

[42]Much of the material in the following section is
derived from an article by V. Coutant and V. Eichenlaub,
"The De Ventis of Theophrastus: Its Contributions to the
Theory of Winds" Bulletin, American Meteorological Society, December, 1974, Spp. 1454-1462.

[43]Harold Cherniss, Aristotle's Criticism of Presocratic Philosophy, Octagon Books Inc., New York, 1964,
p. 127.

motion. Cherniss[44] points out that Aristotle mistakenly
believed that the later Presocratics, who adhered to the
theory that wind is air in motion, also believed that
clouds and rain were compressed air, a view held only by
Anaximenes. This led Aristotle to refute the idea of
wind as air in motion, since for him wind and water could
not be of the same material substrate.[45]

The double anathymiasis was introduced in Meteorologica 360a 7-12. Air was composed of both exhalations,
the moist-cold and the dry-warm (360b 21-25). The heat
of the sun raised the exhalations, but when the dry-warm
exhalation rose aloft, the moist-cold exhalation cooled,
condensed, and fell as rain (360b 20-25). Sometimes one
exhalation prevailed, sometimes the other; consequently,
in some years it could be windy and dry, if the warm-dry
exhalation prevailed, or rainy and wet, if the cold-moist
exhalation prevailed (360b 21-35), and while the sun
could cause winds by raising the warm-dry exhalation, it
could also prevent or hinder winds by stifling the exhalation. Thus stoppages or calms might occur in cold
weather, when the exhalation was not produced, and in
extremely hot weather when the exhalation was quenched
(361b 14-20). Winds blew horizontally, although the exhalation rose vertically, because of the motion of the
celestial sphere (361a 20-30). Thus the winds had their
origin from below, but the motion came from above. Winds

---

[44]Cherniss, p. 128.

[45]cf. Böker, 2243. He feels that the ancients
were conditioned to believe in the separation of air into
the light and heavy. With air, according to Aristotle,
consisting of a mixture between the cold-moist and warm-
dry exhalation, the moist of the vapor eliminated the dry
of the smoke, and the warm of the smoke eliminated the
cold of the vapor. The warm (light) winds were moved
while the moist (heavy) clouds and moisture stood still
or fell out. Thus the matter of air and winds was perceived as different.

were formed by the gradual collection of small quantities
of the exhalation in the same way that rivers formed when
the earth was wet    (361b 1-5).

The warm-dry exhalation presented a handy mechanism for the refutation of the sea-of-air concept of the
Presocratics[46] which insisted that all winds were one,
and for the individualizing of winds, a fundamental concept which permeates the Meteorologica. By making the
warm-dry exhalation the material of wind, and having air
composed of a mixture of the warm-dry and cold-moist exhalation, Aristotle removed the possibility of consider-
ing wind as air in motion, thus convertible into cloud
and water (as he felt the older thinkers believed).
Additionally, the warm-dry exhalation, rising from many
places on the surface of the earth, made possible the
individualization of the winds in contradistinction to
the sea-of-air theory of the older philosophers. Hence,
the warm-dry exhalation dominated Aristotle's etiology,
even in the face of empirical evidence which questioned
the very basis of his system. It gave unity to his anemology, and was inextricably linked with a transcendental
movens (the circularly moving outermost body).[47] The dry
exhalation performed an integrating function for his

---

[46]Cherniss, p. 127 states that the view of "one-
ness" of winds, with only apparent differences due to
the regions from which they blow agrees with that elsewhere attributed to Anaximenes.

[47]This was the outer boundary of the material universe. Its motion from east to west corresponded to the
daily rotation of the earth, in the geocentric world of
Aristotle. Böker, 2227, comments that Aristotle contest-
ed the kinetic gas theory of Democritus, that is, deriva-
tion of movement by internal impulse. His polemicising
against the doctrine of internal movement led to attri-
buting horizontal motion to the celestial sphere and in-
dicated he had little conception of horizontal pressure
differences, an idea approached in De Ventis.

meteorological beliefs, since its activities and affec-
tivities accounted for many of the phenomena in, on, and
about the earth: winds, and also earthquakes, thunder-
bolts, thunder, shooting stars etc.,[48] and in the De La-
pidibus of Theophrastus, the generation of minerals.[49]

His was a largely speculative anemology, heretical
in part, and yet strongly conditioned by the scientific
and philosophical thought of the Presocratics. Aristotle's attempt at a unified wind theory fell short of the
mark, for if the dry exhalation was a convenient basis
for his polemics against the older philosophers, it certainly also presented problems. If the warm-dry exhalation was the material of the winds, how then did cold,
moist winds occur? In coping with this difficulty, Aristotle was forced to place the dry exhalation in the vague
role of a motor, thus stultifying his objection to wind
as air in motion. If the horizontal motion was determined by the turning of the celestial sphere, the problem of explaining the origin of west winds was posed.
Contradictions and exceptions were sprinkled throughout
the Meteorologica, some ignored, others loosely explained, none seeming to distract the author from the occasionally imperious generalizations on which the treatise
is developed.

B. The De Ventis

Numerous parallelisms to the Meteorologica appear
throughout the De Ventis. At the same time the refuta-
tions appear subtly, by omission, by an inductive approach based on more extensive and detailed observations

---

[48]Aristotle, Meteorologica, I-III.

[49]Eichholz, p. 141.

of both the ordinary and extraordinary, and by the will-
ingness to accept a multiplicity of causes for what was,
in Aristotle's view, a unified and integrated system
headed by the doctrine of the double anathymiasis.[50]
The observational examples are the basis for a more inductive formulation of theory, although such is not the
expressed purpose of the work.

Theophrastus does not wish to depart radically
from Aristotle's views. Only in Section 29 is there a
strident clash with Aristotelian concepts. Here Theophrastus flatly states: "But the movement of air is
wind," in direct contradiction to a major tenet of Aristotle. The statement carries serious implications, however, for with the rejection of this keystone many other
tenets of the Aristotelian system crumble. For example,
the warm-dry exhalation, an innovation which stemmed from
Aristotle's rejection of wind as air in motion, is left
without a raison d'etre. The omission of any clear-cut
reference to the role of the dry exhalation in De Ventis
indicates that Theophrastus realizes that the utility of
the innovation had been lost, since it is beset with
mounting problems as the empirical data accumulate.

Theophrastus consequently becomes a more conserv-
ative commentator on what was, in essence, a radical and
dogmatic approach to the explanation of winds. The De
Ventis is less speculative in nature than the Meteorologica, while at the same time attempting to remain systematic. The disjointed condition of these lecture notes
is chiefly responsible for the failure to realize this
purpose. The adherence to detailed facts, and the reso-
lution to avoid speculation are often expressed by the
phrase "this needs to be looked into" (Sections 14, 17,

--------

[50]Hans Strohm, "Zur Meteorologie des Theophrast,"
Philologus, 92 (1937) pp. 249-268; 401-428.

and 25), which typifies Theophrastus' unwillingness to
be bound by a dogmatic, deductive system.


    The Individuality of Winds and Hydrologic Analo-
gies: Section 1 of De Ventis, by stressing the individual nature of the several winds, indicates that Theophrastus is in agreement with Aristotle's refutation of
the sea-of-air concept of the Presocratics.[51] The concept of individualization of winds and their effects permeates the treatise and provides a framework for the development of a Theophrastean anemology. Each wind is
accompanied by clear-cut features and weather effects.
When winds change, they do so by an orderly and pre-
scribed plan (Section 52).

    As in the Meteorologica, a convenient analogy to
rivers and streams can be made from the recognition of
the individual character of winds. Rivers have definite
and distinct sources and termini, as winds must have.
Because the De Ventis is much longer than comparable sections of the Meteorologica, it is possible for Theophrastus to make more of the hydrologic analogy, and so indeed
he does. In relating the strength of a wind to its proximity to the source, Theophrastus (Sections 5 and 6) is
echoing the Meteorologica, 361b 1-5. He compares the
force of a wind moving through a narrow passage to the
rush of water through a gap (Sections 3 and 29). And he
compares the dividing of a wind by an obstacle to the
dividing of a current of water passing around an obstacle
(Section 20). In Section 8, a parallel to the flow of

---

    [51]cf. Meteorologica, 349a 19-32. " . . . and for
this reason some people, wishing to be clever, say that
all winds are one and the same whole, and only seem to
differ, without differing in reality, because of the various places from which the current comes on different
occasions: which is like supposing that all rivers are
but one river." The hydrologic analogy follows.

water is implied. In Section 26, the interchange between land and sea breezes is compared to the inflow and ebb of water. Air, like water, concentrates in hollows, but is diffuse in open areas. And wind is air in motion. It does not appear that Theophrastus is at variance with Aristotle on comparisons of wind to the behavior of water, but rather he develops the concept and gives it more scope. The analogy is not merely for the sake of illustration, but is intended as a parallel, with some of the same causes.

The Mechanical Interplay of Winds: Despite the concurrence on individualism of winds and hydrologic analogies, the innovative contributions of Theophrastus unfold as the treatise is carefully examined. That the occurrence of land and sea breezes was well known to the ancient Greeks is indisputable.[52] Theophrastus is strongly influenced by observations of land and sea breezes. Aristotle theorized that they were rebound winds, that is, a reflux from such obstacles as islands or coastal hills. For him this was a necessary solution to explain the phenomena, as winds were caused by the warm-dry exhalation, and no such exhalation could arise at sea.

The Theophrastean viewpoint appears at first similar, but there is a fundamental difference. For Theophrastus, land and sea breezes arise through concentrations of cold air, and through a mechanical interchange (Section 26). Whereas the dry exhalation was critical to Aristotle, it is an unnecessary adjunct for Theophrastus, and winds can originate from cold and moist areas (Section 24). Thus for Theophrastus, the build-up of

---

[52]J. Neumann, "The Sea and Land Breezes in the Classical Greek Literature," Bulletin, American Meteorological Society, Vol. 54, 1973, pp. 5-8.

cold air and the subsequent mechanical exchange is in-
strumental in causing the reversal, while the obstacles
of terrain serve more or less as containers or restric-
tive enclosures rather than cause a rebound. This recognition of a mechanical interplay within the atmosphere
gives order and system to Theophrastus' approach to wind
theory. It is extended to the off-land winds (those
winds which come from the open sea and are thus thought
different from reversing winds, or sea breezes) (Section
53), to the diurnal features of winds (Section 53), and,
by extension, to an explanation of the general circulation itself, as manifested by the dominance of north and
south winds at Athens.

This seemingly dichotomous division of primary
winds in Greece leads Theophrastus to extend his theories
of land and sea breeze behavior to the larger scale of
the general circulation.[53] The explanation for the dominance of north and south winds is Aristotelian, to be
sure (Section 2, cf. Meteorologica, 361a 5-10), and yet
the interchange process is innovative, occurring without
reference to the exhalations which were critical to
Aristotle's explanation, and brings Theophrastus close
to, but not within grasp of, the concept of horizontal
pressure gradients. The air is compressed by the power
of the sun to the north and south of its path, and in
consequence of strong condensation on both sides, the
winds become stronger and more persistent. This idea of
a mechanical reciprocating exchange in the atmosphere is
extended to rains and other phenomena in Section 48.

Unfortunately, Theophrastus then falls victim to
some of the deductive traps which plague Aristotle and

---

[53] cf. Böker, 2240 and 2332 for historical background on theories of the ancients in explanation of the
prevalence of north and south winds in the Aegean area.

the Meteorologica, including the winds of Egypt and the
occurrence of winter etesians. As the reciprocating
interchange occurs, the regions in proximity to the more
northern regions, including Greece, should have more frequent and forceful north winds, following the analogy to
hydrology. But: "For those who live in Egypt and nearby
the situation is reversed" (Section 5). The south wind
should be more frequent and forceful. Theophrastus still
adheres to the Aristotelian conception of etesians resulting from the melting of far northern snows (Meteorologica, 361b 15-20). Yet his mechanistic approach to
atmospheric behavior would call for a reciprocating flow
of air from the south during the winter, which failed to
occur. He resolves the dilemma by reference to the leuconotoi, white south winds of spring (Section 11), which
like a river far from its source, have a flow which is
weak and indefinite, and difficult to discern.

Reduced Role of Dry Exhalation and Horizontal
Motion of Winds: The acceptance that winds are cold and
moist, stemming from observations of land and sea breezes,
greatly diminishes the role of the Aristotelian warm-dry
exhalation while at the same time supporting a much
stronger role for the vaporization of the cold-moist.[54]

---

[54]Hans Strohm, "Zur Meteorologie des Theophrastus,
p. 258, note 19. Strohm states that for Aristotle the
air was always counted as warm. Theophrastus' innovation
"air . . . cold and vaporous" (Section 19) which resulted
from a study of off-land and reverse winds was not a ge-
neric characteristic, but significant in the history of
the problem. Strohm feels that the exhalation still
plays a role in Theophrastus' anemology, but only as it
exerts an effect like warmth in general without representing in any way the body and matter of wind. In Section 40 Theophrastus states in reference to the west
wind, which blows off vaporizing water: "For it does not
await the heat as on land, but moves around because it is
passing over water." Here Theophrastus departs from

In fact, the much diminished role of exhalations in the treatise is striking. They, (or it, for the expression occurs only in the singular) are mentioned only in Sections 15 and 23. In Section 15, the exhalation (presumably the warm-dry exhalation) seems to have precedence over the sun, but doubts are raised forthwith.

The sun, then, becomes increasingly important. It is mentioned 20 times, in no slighting fashion. This corresponds to the dominant role of the sun assigned in Section 5 of the De Igne.[55] The action of the sun, for all practical purposes, takes over the role of the dry exhalation while maintaining its older role.

Conceding a role for the cold and moist exhalation allows Theophrastus to equate wind with air in motion, which was flatly renounced by Aristotle. Hence his theories represent a return to the older ideas of the Presocratics. In thus equating wind to air in motion, Theophrastus is able to solve the problem of horizontal motion of air without the aid of the transcendental primum movens educed by Aristotle. The mechanism of horizontal motion is transferred to the immanent nature of the air itself, a resultant of two forces. (Section 22) This crude analogy to the meteorological concept of hydrostatic equilibrium alleviates the Aristotelian shortcoming, reliance on a one-tracked directional mechanism, in explanation of the horizontal motion of the wind.

Advective Properties of Winds and Local Temperature Differences: Perceptive insights into localized

---

Aristotelian doctrine, which cannot explain the motion of saturated moisture-laden breezes. Theophrastus' new idea is that these can go into motion by themselves.

[55] Victor Coutant, Theophrastus De Igne, Royal Van Gorcum, Assen, 1971, xxvi and 72 pp.

heating processes are combined with an imaginative approach to advection (horizontal heat transfer) to allow
Theophrastus to overcome one of the major shortcomings of
the Aristotelian approach. If winds result from the horizontal motion of the warm-dry exhalation, as Aristotle
believed, how then does one account for the varying temperatures of winds, or of different areas? Theophrastus,
unencumbered by the restrictions of the dry anathymiasis,
combines a favorite, but unfortunate, trick of the ancients (the breath analogy), with some new insights of
his own.

The breath analogy arose through observations of
the blowing of the breath on the hand. It felt cooler,
but the effect was only physiological. The Greeks, however, adhered to the idea that winds passing through constrictions were cooled.[56]

Theophrastus rewrites the breath equation in a new
form.[57] If the wind is warm, coming from a wide opening
and in a goodly amount, it remains warm like the breath
issuing from an open mouth. If, however, the wind is
forced through a constriction, the temperature concurs
with that of the air encountered, either warm or cold
(Section 20). Thus the temperature of any region is the
sum of characteristics locally acquired and of those ad-
vected (Section 21). In this approach, then, Theophrastus stands on the verge of a true understanding of horizontal temperature contrasts.

---

[56]Böker, 2231 comments that the obviously false
theory that air subjected to compression becomes cold,
while that which expands becomes hot, prevented the
ancients from recognizing thermal differences as the
causes for winds.

[57]H. Strohm, "Zur Meteorologie des Theophrast,"
p. 252.

Conditioning Factors: Theophrastus is acutely
aware of topography in affecting the direction, force,
and characteristics of winds (Section 29). The effects
of constrictions, mountains, passes, and high bluffs in
modifying the winds are discussed in detail. In addition, the effects of topographic obstacles in generating
orographic rainfall are noted (Section 5).

Along with the conditioning role of topography,
Theophrastus recognizes that the seasonal temperature
differential between land surfaces and surrounding water
bodies modifies the characteristics of winds. Thus the
west wind, blowing from the Atlantic and Mediterranean,
is warm in winter and cold in summer (Section 43). Winds
with large fetches are likely to arrive in Greece moisture-laden and humid, as is the case of the west wind
(Section 42). The south wind is fair in Africa, but, becoming modified with passage over the Mediterranean, "is
always rainier in districts farther away" (Section 7).
The contrasting seasonal capabilities of land and sea in
inducing cloud formation (Section 60) are additional conditioning factors, although his explanation has shortcomings. Both Theophrastus and Aristotle associate cloud
formation with coldness and of course have no conception
of the role of adiabatic cooling. Thus the paradox of
the cloud which forms over the sea in winter (which is
warmer than the land). It is to be feared, because the
force which formed it must have been very powerful to
overcome the warmth (relatively) of the sea. Conversely,
the land cloud in the summer (when the land is warmer)
must be feared, because it results from a powerful force
to overcome the warmth of the land.

C.  Conclusions

In spite of a general concurrence with Aristote-

lian doctrine, including insistence on the individualism
of winds and refutation of the sea-of-air concept, the
De Ventis contains a number of significant innovations,
and suggests that the author comes close to an understanding of several important meteorological concepts.
The relegation, mostly by omission, of the Aristotelian
warm-dry exhalation to a minor role in his etiology allows Theophrastus to redirect his anemology to the Presocratic concept of wind as air in motion, whereas Aristotle's renunciation of this idea had directed the understanding of winds a step backward into speculative meta-
physics.

Relieved of the burden of the dry exhalation,
Theophrastus is able to conceive of a more mechanical
approach to wind behavior which bespeaks an inkling of
understanding of atmospheric pressure. The acceptance
of winds as cold and moist, following from observations
of sea breezes and local winds, opens the way for new
theories of advection and the correct interpretation of
horizontal temperature differences. The causes for horizontal motion of the winds are removed from the transcendental movens of Aristotle and attributed to the nature of the air itself. Relying upon a keen observational base, De Ventis reveals perceptive comments concerning climatic change and the physiological effects of
climate, while the role of orography in modifying wind
systems and in creating fallwinds and local winds is ful-
ly appreciated.

Although Theophrastus falls into some of the same
deductive traps to which Aristotle fell victim, the greater empiricism of the De Ventis and the increased reliance
on an inductive approach contrast with the earlier work
of Aristotle. We view Theophrastus on his own merits, a
careful thinker, bound to some extent by the doctrines of
Aristotle and the Peripatetics, but also innovative in

several respects.

## IV.  The Windrose of Theophrastus

The windrose represents, in diagram form, the circle of the horizon, on which fixed points or arcs are assigned specific wind names.  These are often connected by radii to the central point, at which the observer is stationed.  All windroses have a north-south axis, representing the meridian of the observer.  Other wind names, however, may have only a superficial conformance to compass directions.

Böker, 2335-2342, in an historical summary of the development of the Greek windrose, points out that, until Aristotle's time, the Greeks were not acquainted with a genuine windrose, but rather utilized a more or less systematic distribution of the points of origin of the winds on the horizon for the purpose of geographical orientation.  The centralization of the lines of wind direction in the center of the horizon circle was apparently, in older times, not so much a matter of course as it seems to us today, according to Böker.

We take the windrose of Theophrastus to be identical with that of Aristotle.  While differing in other respects with the master, Theophrastus offers no windrose of his own and in all points he uses the same wind directions as Aristotle, never altering but only supplementing.  Other particulars of winds tally between the two authorities.  Thus we are able to draw the windrose of Theophrastus by using the directions given by Aristotle in Meteorologica II, 6, and adding material appearing here and there in the De Ventis.

Aristotle's instructions are, briefly: (1) draw the circle of the horizon for the sake of clarity.  (2) draw the diameter from A, which is the equinoctial sunset, to B, the equinoctial sunrise.  (3) let another diameter cut this at right angles, with the point H being

the north and O being the south. (4) draw the diameter
from Z the summer sunrise, to Γ the winter sunset, and
the diameter from Δ the winter sunrise to E the summer
sunset. (5) points I and K divide the remainder of the
quadrants into equal sections. Draw the chord I-K,
which corresponds closely to the ever-visible circle,
but not exactly.

Now the names of the winds may be determined in
reference to the points on the circle of the horizon.
Zephyros blows from A, and its opposite Apeliotes blows
from B. Boreas or Aparctias blows from H, and its opposite Notos, blows from O. Caecias blows from Z and its
opposite, Lips, blows from Γ . Eurus blows from Δ and
its opposite Argestes or Olympias blows from E. Thras-
cias, blowing from I and Meses from K have no opposites
except for a local wind, Phoenicias, which blows from N.

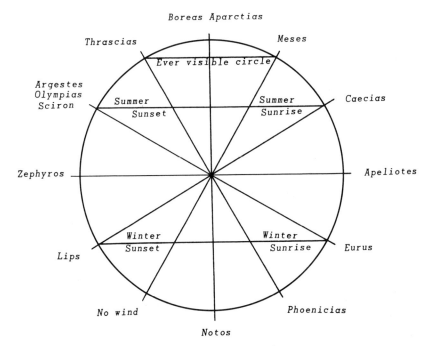

Figure 3. Aristotle's windrose.

Our depiction of Aristotle's windrose shows a symmetrical representation, following the Wood-Symons translation of De Ventis and D'arcy Wentworth Thompson.[58] That is, we assume that when Aristotle says summer sunrise, he refers to the direction of sunrise at the summer solstice as seen from an observer at Athens, $30^\circ$ $50$'[59] or approximately $30^\circ$ from the equinoctial sunrise. Thus the windrose would be divided into 12 equal segments of $30^\circ$ each.

Thompson's viewpoint is opposed by Böker, who states that Aristotle's use of the earth-sphere in contrast to the Ionic flat-earth concept, and his development geometrically of a drum-shaped oikoumene (inhabited area) by means of a central projection (projection point located at the center of the earth-sphere) would dictate that his conception of "summer sunrise" would represent the angular departure from the equinoctial sunrise as seen from an observer at the equator rather than at the latitude of Athens.[60] Thus Böker's interpretation of Aristotle's windrose places Caecias at $24^\circ$ from Apeliotes

---

[58]D'arcy Wentworth Thompson, "The Greek Winds" The Classical Review, May-June 1918, pp. 49-56.

[59]Given by sin x = sin w cosec s where w is the angle of the ecliptic ($23^\circ$ $51$' in Aristotle's day) s is the co-latitude (or $90^\circ$-$37^\circ$ $58$') of Athens, and x is the solstitial azimuth required.

[60]The geometric considerations of this concept are developed in Meteorologica II, v. 362b ff, immediately preceding his discussion of the windrose. The angle from the equinoctial position as seen from an observer at the equator would be the ecliptic angle, $23^\circ$ $51$' (in Aristotle's time), or approximately $24^\circ$.

and Meses at $57°$ from Apeliotes.[61]

Both Thompson and Böker forward convincing arguments for their varying interpretations. The De Ventis presents no information which allows us to confirm either viewpoint. Therefore, for want of sufficient evidence to the contrary, we use, as Theophrastus' windrose, a horizon circle with divisions at approximately $30°$, based on the solstitial positions of the sun at sunrise and sunset as seen from an observer at Athens. This windrose could be used throughout much of the known world with only minor variations of the midsummer sunrise, the divisions still approximate one-third of the quadrant, and they fulfill an aesthetic and mathematical desire for a symmetrical windrose diagram.

---

[61]Aristotle then divided the remaining portion of the quadrant into two equal portions, $33°$ of arc each. $(\frac{90°-24°}{2})$.

# BIBLIOGRAPHY

Works Related to Contemporary Climates
of Greece and the Aegean

Hannes An der Lan, "Meteorologische Besonderheiten der
 Ägäis" Archiv Fur Meteorologie, Geophysik und Bioclimatologie, Band I (1949), 288-409.


Erwin R. Biel, Climatology of the Mediterranean Area,
 Univ. of Chicago, Institute of Meteorology, Misc.
 Repts., No. 13 (1944).


Glenn W. Brier, "Diurnal and Semidiurnal Tides in Relation to Precipitation Variations" Monthly Weather
 Review, Vol. 93, 1965, pp. 93-100.


Leon N. Carapiperis, The Etesian Winds Part VI, On the
 Daily Variation of the Velocity of the Etesian Winds
 in Athens, Athens, 1964, Ethnikon Asteroskopeion
 Hypomnemata Ser. II, Meteorologica, No. 17.


Leon N. Carapiperis, "On the Periodicity of the Etesians
 in Athens," Weather Vol. VI, 1951, pp. 378-379.


Great Britain, Meteorological Office, Weather in the Mediterranean, 2nd Ed., Vol. I, London, 1964.


J. Griffiths, (ed.) Climates of Africa, Vol. 10 of World
 Survey of Climatology, Elsevier Publishing Co., New
 York, 1972.


W. E. Howell and P. P. Karapiperis, Interpretation of the
 Rainfall Climate of Marathon, Greece, Publisher un-
 known, Athens, 1952.


W. Kendrew, Climates of the Continents, 3rd Ed., Oxford
 University Press, New York, 1942.


E. G. Mariolopoulos, An Outline of the Climate of Greece,
 Publications of the Meteorological Institute of the
 University of Athens, #6, Athens, 1961.

D. A. Metaxas, A Contribution to the Study of Etesian Winds, Presented at the Mediterranean Meteorological Conference, Norfolk, Virginia, June 1970.

Glenn T. Trewartha, An Introduction to Climate, 4th Edition, McGraw-Hill, New York, 1968.

Works Related to Past Climates
of Greece and the Aegean

C. E. P. Brooks, Climate Through the Ages, McGraw-Hill, New York, 1949.

Leon N. Carapiperis, The Etesian Winds, I. The Opinions of the Ancient Greeks on the Etesian Winds, Ethnikon Asterokospeion Hypomnemata Ser. II, Meteorologica, No. 9, Athens, 1962.

Rhys Carpenter, Discontinuity in Greek Civilization (The J. H. Gray lectures for 1965) University Press, Cambridge, 1966.

B. Frenzel, "Climatic Change in the Atlantic/Sub-Boreal Transition on the Northern Hemisphere" Proceedings of the International Symposium on World Climate from 8000 B.C. to 0 A.D., J. S. Sawyer, (ed.) Royal Meteorological Society, London, 1966, pp. 99-123.

H. H. Lamb, The Changing Climate, Methuen and Co., London, 1966.

H. H. Lamb, "The New Look of Climatology" Nature, Vol. 223, 1969, pp. 1209-1214.

H. H. Lamb, "Climatic Changes During the Course of Early Greek History" Antiquity, Vol. 42, 1968, pp. 231-233.

H. H. Lamb, "On the Nature of Certain Climatic Epochs Which Differed from the Modern (1900-39) Normal" Changes of Climate-Proceedings of Rome Symposium UNESCO and WMO, 1963, pp. 125-149.

H. H. Lamb, R. P. W. Lewis, and A. Woodroffe, "Atmospheric Circulation and Main Climatic Variables between 8000 B.C. and 0 B.C.: Meteorological Evidence" Proceedings of the International Symposium on World Climate 8000 to 0 B.C., J. S. Sawyer (ed.) Royal Meteorological Society, London, pp. 174-217.

L. Starkel, "Post-glacial Climate and the Moulding of European Relief" Proceedings of the International Symposium on World Climate 8000 to 0 B.C., J. S. Sawyer (ed.) Royal Meteorological Society, London, pp. 15-33.

## Works Related to De Ventis and
## to Ancient Meteorology

Harold Cherniss, Aristotle's Criticism of Presocratic Philosophy, Octagon Books Inc., New York, 1964, (Originally 1935 by Johns Hopkins Press).

J. Neumann, "The Sea and Land Breezes in the Classical Greek Literature" Bulletin, American Meteorological Society, Vol. 54, 1973, pp. 5-8.

D'arcy Wentworth Thompson, "The Greek Winds," Classical Review, May-June 1918, pp. 49-56.

## Data Sources Consulted

Data Processing Division, USAF ETAC Air Weather Service (MAC) Revised Uniform Summary of Surface Weather Observations, Athens, Greece.

Egypt, Meteorological Department, Climatological Normals for Egypt, C. Tsoumas, Cairo, 1950.

Egypt, Ministry of Public Works, Climatological Normals for Egypt and the Sudan, Cyprus, and Palestine, Cairo, 1938.

Weather in the Mediterranean 2nd Edition, Vol. II, Great Britain, Meteorological Office, London, 1964.

Koninklijk Nederlands Meteorologisch Instituut De Bilt, Marine Climatological Summaries for the Mediterranean and Southern Indian Ocean, Vol. 4, 1964, De Bilt, 1972.

Summary of Synoptic Meteorological Observations Mediterranean Marine Areas, Vol. 7, U. S. Naval Weather Service Command, 1970.

Unpublished data made available by Hellenic National Meteorological Service, Athens, and National Climatic Center, Asheville, North Carolina.

# THEOPHRASTUS
# CONCERNING WINDS

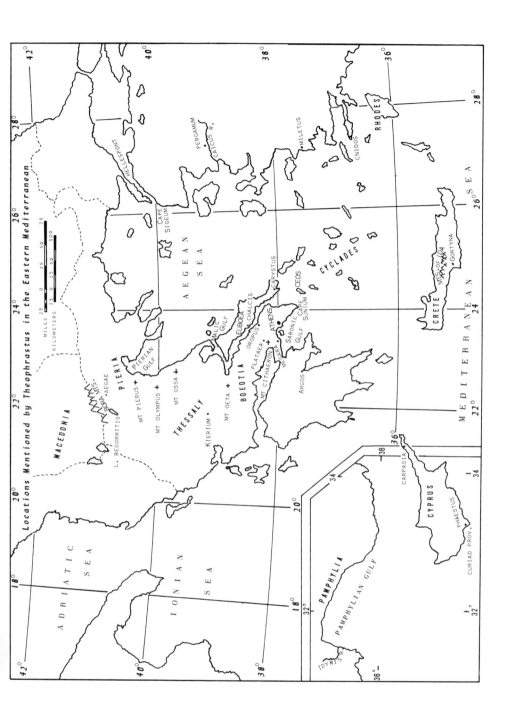

Locations Mentioned by Theophrastus in the Eastern Mediterranean

ADRIATIC SEA

IONIAN SEA

MACEDONIA

L. BEGORRITIS
BORA MTS.
AEGAE
PIERIA
MT PIERUS
MT OLYMPUS
PIERIAN GULF

THESSALY
KIERIUM
MT OSSA
MT OETA
MALIC GULF

BOEOTIA
CHALCIS
EUBOEA
PLATAEA
OROPUS
MT CITHAERON
MEGARA
ATHENS
SARONIC GULF
CAPE SUNIUM
CEOS
CARYSTUS

ARGOS

CAPE SIGEUM

AEGEAN SEA

CYCLADES

HELLESPONT

PERGAMUM
CAICUS R.

CNIDOS

MILETUS

RHODES

CRETE
MTS. OF IDA
GORTYNA
PHAESTUS

MEDITERRANEAN SEA

PAMPHYLIA
PAMPHYLIAN GULF
IDYRIS

CYPRUS
CARPASIA
CURIAD PROV.

MILES
KILOMETERS
25  0  25  50  75
25  0  25  50  75  100

# ΠΕΡΙ ΑΝΕΜΩΝ

1.  Ἡ τῶν ἀνέμων φύσις, ἐκ τίνων μὲν καὶ πῶς καὶ διὰ τί-
νας αἰτίας γίνεται, τεθεώρηται πρότερον. ὅτι δ'ἑκάστοις αἱ
δυνάμεις καὶ ὅλως τὰ παρακολουθοῦντα κατὰ λόγον ἀκολουθεῖ
πειρᾶσθαι χρὴ λέγειν, οἷσπερ σχεδὸν διαφέρουσιν ἀλλήλων.
αἱ γὰρ διαφοραὶ περὶ ταῦτα καὶ ἐν τούτοις, οἷον μέγεθος,
μικρότης, ψυχρότης, θερμότης, ⟨καὶ⟩ ἁπλῶς τὸ χειμερινὸν
'ἢ εὐδιεινὸν, καὶ ὑέτιον 'ἢ αἴθριον· ἔτι δὲ τὸ πολλάκις
'ἢ ὀλιγάκις, καθ' ὥραν 'ἢ τὸ μὴ ἀεὶ πνεῖν, καὶ συνεχεῖς
καὶ ὁμαλεῖς 'ἢ διαλείποντας καὶ ἀνωμαλεῖς· καὶ ὅλως 'ἃ
συμβαίνει περὶ τὸν οὐρανὸν 'ἢ περὶ τὸν ἀέρα καὶ τὴν γῆν
καὶ τὴν θάλατταν διὰ τὴν πνοήν. ὡς γὰρ ⌊ἂν⌋ ἁπλῶς εἰπεῖν,
ἐν τούτοις καὶ περὶ ταῦτα τυγχάνουσιν αἱ ζητήσεις ἐν οἷς
καὶ τὰ περὶ τῶν ζῴων καὶ φυτῶν ἐμπεριλαμβάνεται.

2.  ἐπεὶ δ' ἑκάστου τόπος ἴδιος ὑπόκειται καὶ τοῦθ' ὥσπερ τῆς οὐσίας, ἀπὸ τούτου, ὡς ἁπλῶς εἰπεῖν, καὶ αἱ διαφοραὶ καὶ αἱ δυνάμεις αἱ ἑκάστων [εἰπεῖν]· οἷον πρῶτον ἡ
τοῦ μεγέθους καὶ σμικρότητος καὶ ψυχρότητος καὶ θερμότητος, καὶ πλήθους καὶ ὀλιγότητος, καὶ τῶν ἄλλων τῶν πλείστων. ὑπάρχει δὲ ταὐτὰ τὰ δ' ἐναντία τοῖς ἐναντίοις· ἀμφότερα δ' εὐλόγως· οἷον τῷ βορέᾳ καὶ τῷ νότῳ· μεγάλοι μὲν
γὰρ ἄμφω καὶ πλεῖστον χρόνον πνέουσι, διὰ τὸ συνωθεῖσθαι
πλεῖστον ἀέρα πρὸς ἄρκτον καὶ μεσημβρίαν, πλαγίων ὄντων
πρὸς τὴν τοῦ ἡλίου φορὰν τὴν ἀπ' ἀνατολῶν ἐπὶ δυσμάς·ἐξω-
θεῖται γὰρ ἐνταῦθα τῇ τοῦ ἡλίου δυνάμει. διὸ καὶ πυκνότα-
τος καὶ συννεφέστατος ὁ ἀήρ· ἀθροιζομένου δ' ἐφ' ἑκάτερα
πολλοῦ, καὶ πλείων ἡ ῥύσις καὶ συνεχεστέρα γίνεται πλεονά-

APPARATUS
1.1.διαφέρει MSS. διαφέρουσιν MARGO VASCOSANI  6. ⟨καὶ⟩
μικρ. VASCOSANUS ⟨καὶ⟩ ἁπλῶς SCHNEIDER IV 680 τὸν χ. VAS.
7. αἴθριον L ALDUS, SCHN. I αἰθέριον CETT.  9. αἰωμαλεῖς
VAS.  11. ⌊ἂν⌋ CORAY, SCHN. V 159  12. ἐμπεριλαμβάνεται
MSS.,WIMMER περιλαμβάνεται VAS., FURLANUS 75

2. 1.τοῦτ'FURL. 75  2. τῆς οὐσίας SC. αὐτῶν κοινὸν BONA-
VENTURA (C) τούτων MSS. τούτου TURNEBUS, MAR.VAS. οἷς MSS.

3

1. We have earlier considered the nature of the winds:
of what they consist, in what way they come to be, and
by what they are caused. We must now try to explain
that each wind is systematically accompanied by effects
and in general by phenomena whereby the winds are dif-
ferentiated from one another. These differences refer
to matters like force, temperature, storm or calm, and
(speaking loosely) rain or fair weather, frequency (or
rarity), seasonal occurrence or failure, continuous and
consistent or discontinuous and irregular. In fact,
what happens in the sky, in the air, on earth and on
the sea is due to the wind. And to put it briefly,
our inquiries deal with matters which also concern the
life and well-being of plants and animals.

2. Since each wind has its own proper place and this
fact is, as it were, a part of its nature, from this,
to put it simply, are derived the differences and the
powers of each, such as force, temperature, amount, and
most other qualities. Opposing winds have both opposing qualities and the same qualities, and rightly so.
Example: the north wind and the south wind are strong
winds and blow the longest time, because most air is
forced to the north and to the south, since both districts are athwart the motion of the sun from east to
west. The air there is dislodged outwards by the
effect of the sun. This accounts for the extreme density and cloudiness of the air. It is collected in
quantity on both sides, so that the flow is greater,

ὡς BON.    3. δυνάμεις ἕκαστον MSS. ⟨καὶ⟩ ἔκ. HEINSIUS,
SCHN. I καὶ τὰ καθ' ἕκ. SCHN. IV 681 αἱ καθ' ἕκ. WI. ἑκάστων BURNIKEL 24 [εἰπεῖν]WI. 6. ὑπάρχει δὲ ταῦτα MSS. τὰ
μὲν ὑπάρχει δὲ ταὐτὰ ⟨τοῖς μὲν⟩ ὑπάρχει ταὐτὰ SCHN. I τὸ
νότῳ BASILIENSIS  9. πρὸς ἄρκτον...ὄντων OM. HEINS. πλαγ-
ίους ὄντας VEL πλάγια ὄντα TURN.    10. ἐξωθεῖσθαι MSS.
ἐξωθεῖται MAR.VAS.   12. συνεχέστατος M συνεφέστατος CETT.

κις· ἀφ' ὧν τά τε μεγέθη καὶ συνέχεια καὶ τὸ πλῆθος αὐτῶν
καὶ ἄλλο τοιοῦτόν ἐστιν.

3. ἡ δὲ ψυχρότης καὶ θερμότης ἐμφανέστατα δόξαιεν 'ἂν
εἶναι διὰ τοὺς τόπους γινόμεναι. ψυχρὰ γὰρ τὰ πρὸς ἄρκτον,
τὰ δὲ πρὸς μεσημβρίαν ἀλεεινά, τὸ δ' ἀφ' ἑκατέρων ῥέον ὅ-
μοιον. ἅμα γὰρ καὶ ἧττον ἀναπεπταμένον τὸ σύνεγγυς καὶ μὴ
ἀναπεπταμένη ⟨ἡ⟩ φορά· τὸ δὲ διὰ στενοῦ καὶ σφοδροτέρως
φερόμενον ψυχρότερον, τὸ δ' εἰς τὸ πόρρω διακεχυμένον μᾶλλον καὶ ἀνειμένον. διὸ καὶ ὁ νότος ἐκεῖ ψυχρότερος 'ἢ παρ'
ἡμῖν, ὡς δέ τινές φασι, καὶ μᾶλλον 'ἢ βορέας. ποιεῖ δέ τι
καὶ μεταβολὴ πρὸς φαντασίαν, ἀλεεινοῦ προυπάρχοντος τοῦ
τόπου.

4. καὶ τοῦτο μὲν κοινόν, ὡς εἰπεῖν, πᾶσι. τὸ δ' ὑέτιον
καὶ αἴθριον ἑκατέρου καὶ τὸ κυματῶδες καὶ ἄκυμον καὶ πυκνὸν καὶ συνεχὲς καὶ ἀνωμαλὲς καὶ ὅμαλον, ἔτι δὲ τὸ μέγεθος
τοῦ μὲν ἀρχομένου, τοῦ δὲ λήγοντος, πρὸς τὴν ἀπόστασιν τῶν
τόπων ἀποδίδοται μᾶλλον. ὅθεν μὲν γὰρ ἕκαστος πνεῖ, παρ'
ἐκείνοις αἴθριος· ὅποι δ' ἀπωθεῖ τὸν ἀέρα, παρ' ἐκείνοις
⟨δ'⟩ ἐπινεφὴς καὶ ὑέτιος. διόπερ ὁ μὲν βορέας καὶ μᾶλλον
οἱ ἐτησίαι τοῖς πρὸς μεσημβρίαν καὶ ἀνατολὴν οἰκοῦσιν ὑέ-

---

συννεφέστατα MAR.VAS. συννεφέστατος SCHN. I    14. ἐφ' ὧν
MSS. ἀφ'ὧν TURN.,MAR.VAS.

3. 3. ἀφ' ἑκάτερον MSS. ἀφ' ἑκατέρων TURN.,MAR.VAS. ῥέ-
πον PALMERIUS APUD SCHN. IV 681    4. ἧττον ἀναπεπταμέναι
UZ ἧτ. ἐναναπεπταμέναι CETT. ἧτ. ἀναπεπταμέναι ALD.,TURN.
ἀναπεπταμένον SCHN. I τῷ σύνεγγυς MSS. τὸ σύν. SCHN. I
καὶ ἐναπεπταμένη φορᾷ U ALD.,VAS. καὶ ἀναπεπταμένη φορᾷ
CETT. καὶ ἐναπεπταμένη φορὰ MAR.VAS. καὶ μὴ ἀναπεπταμένη
φορᾷ FURL. 56 καὶ μὴ ἀναπεπταμένη ⟨ἡ⟩ φορὰ SCHN. I VENTUS
ENIM QUI EX PROXIMIS LOCIS ORITUR, QUIA MINUS TRANSIT RE-
GIONEM ET PROPTEREA QUASI PER ANGUSTUM LOCUM VENIT FRIGI-
DUS SPIRAT    BON.    6. ψυχρότερα DLXZ ψυχρότερον CETT.
εἴς τε τὸ MSS. τὸ δ' εἰς τὸ SCHN. I διακεκαυμένον MSS. διακεχυμένον SCHN. I    7.ἀνειμένον L SCHN. I ἀνειμένου CETT.

more continuous, and more frequent. This is the cause
of the force, the continuity, the amount and other such
features of these winds.

3. It seems very clear that the cold and the heat arise
from the geographical source. The lands to the north
are cold, those to the south warm. The winds which flow
from the respective lands are similar. At the same time
the less open the succeeding district, the less diffuse
the movement, so that wind passing through a narrow con-
fine with a greater rush is colder, but that which is
diffused over a greater distance is gentle. Hence the
south wind is colder in the south than in our climate,
some say, and more than the north wind. The change adds
to the sensation if the place was warm already.

4. Generally this holds for all winds. Whether a wind
brings rain or shine, whether it is gusty or steady,
whether it is frequent or continuous, regular or irregular, forceful or weak when it starts and when it drops
away, depends on the distance of the place from which
it blows and that to which it displaces the air. The
former enjoys sunshine, the latter has clouds and rain.
That is why the north wind and, even more, the etesians
are rainy in the south and the east, while the south

---

8. [τι] FURL. 77   9. ἀλλ' εἰ MSS. ἀλλὰ TURN. ἀλεεινοῦ
FURL. 56

4.   2. ἐκάτερον L ALD.,VAS. ἐκατέρου CETT. ἐκατέρων TURN.
MAR.VAS.   4. ἐρχομένου MSS. ἀρχομένου TURN.,MAR.VAS.
ἐπίστασιν MSS. ἀπόστασιν FURL. 56   5. ἀπολύει μᾶλλον L
ALD.,CAMOTIUS ἀποδύει CETT. ἀποκλίνει VEL ἀποδιδοῖ TURN.
⟨ἀποδύει 'ἡ⟩ ἀποδίδοται FURL. 56 [ἀποδύει 'ἡ] SCHN. II
588 ἀποδίδοται μ. WI.   6. ὅπου MSS. QUO PELLIT AEREM
FURL. 56 ὅποι WI. ἀπαθὲς LZ ALD. ἀπαθεῖς CETT. ἀπωθεῖ
TURN.,FURL. 56 τοῦ ἀέρα L τὸν ἀέρα P τὸ ἀ. CETT. [δ']
HEINS.,SCHN. I   9. πως εἰπεῖν MSS. ὥς MAR.VAS. οἱ OM.

τιοι, ὁ δὲ νότος καὶ ὡς ἁπλῶς εἰπεῖν οἱ ἐξ ἐκείνου τοῦ
τόπου πνέοντες τοῖς πρὸς ἄρκτον.

5.  οὐ μικρὰ δ' ἐνταῦθα ἀλλὰ μεγίστη ῥοπὴ τὸ τὰς χώρας ὕ-
ψος ἔχειν· ὅπου γὰρ 'ἀν προσκόψῃ τὰ νέφη καὶ λάβῃ στάσιν,
ἐνταῦθα καὶ ὕδατος γένεσις. διὸ καὶ τῶν σύνεγγυς τόπων ἄλλοι παρ' ἄλλοις ὑέτιοι τῶν ἀνέμων. ἀλλὰ περὶ μὲν ὑδάτων ἐν
ἑτέροις εἴρηται διὰ πλειόνων. ἐκ τῆς αὐτῆς δ' αἰτίας καὶ ὁ
μὲν βορέας εὐθὺς ἀρχόμενος μέγας, ὁ δὲ νότος λήγων. ὅθεν
καὶ ἡ παροιμία συμβουλεύει τὰ περὶ τοὺς πλοῦς. ὁ μὲν γὰρ
εὐθὺς οἷον ἐπικεῖται τοῖς περὶ ἄρκτον οἰκοῦσιν, ὁ δὲ μακρὰν ἀφέστηκε. χρονιωτέρα δ' ἡ τῶν ἄπωθεν ἀπορροὴ, καὶ ὅταν
ἀθροισθῇ πλῆθος. τοῖς γὰρ περὶ Αἴγυπτον καὶ τοὺς τόπους ἐ-
κείνους ἀνάπαλιν ὁ νότος ἀρχόμενος μέγας. ὅθεν καὶ τὴν
παροιμίαν ἐναντίως λέγουσιν.

6.  ὡσαύτως δὲ καὶ τὸ πυκνὸν καὶ ἄκυμον καὶ συνεχὲς καὶ
ὁμαλὲς ἐκείνοις ὁ νότος ποιεῖ μᾶλλον. ἀεὶ γὰρ τοῖς ἐγγὺς
ἕκαστος τοιοῦτος, τοῖς δὲ πόρρω καὶ ἀνωμαλὴς καὶ διεσπασ-
μένος [μᾶλλον]. τούτων μὲν οὖν τὰς εἰρημένας αἰτίας ὑποληπτέον, αἵπερ ἐμφανεῖς καὶ κατ' ἄλλους τόπους εἰσὶν ἐλάττους καὶ ἔλαττον ἀπέχοντας ἀλλήλων. τοῦτο δ' 'ἀν καὶ δόξειεν ἄλογον εἶναι. ὁ μὲν γὰρ νότος ἀεὶ τοῖς ἑαυτοῦ τόποις
αἴθριος, ὁ δὲ βορέας, ὅταν ᾖ χειμὼν μέγας, ἐν μὲν τοῖς
πλησίον συννεφὴς, ἔξω δ' αἴθριος.

EORU νότος καὶ ἁπλῶς εἰπεῖν οἱ ἐξ ἐκείνου τοῦ τόπου πνέοντες SCHN. IV 682   10. τόπου LACUNA 6 LITTERARUM  DIM
PQUXZ τόπου πλέοντες LO ⟨ἄνεμοι⟩ πνέοντες BON. τῇ πρὸς
ἄρκτον CAM.

5.  1. μικρὰν EO SCHN. I μικρὰ CETT. μεγίστη ῥοπὴ MSS.
μεγίστην ῥοπὴν SCHN. I E VERSIONE TURNEBI τῆς M SCHN. I
τὰς CETT.   2. ἔχειν MSS. ἔχει SCHN. I ὅπου 'ἀν DLRXZ
ALD.,SCHN. I ὅπου γὰρ 'ἀν CETT. παρακόψῃ MAR.VAS.,SCHN.
I  E VERS. TURN.

6.  2. [ἐκείνοις] FURL. 78 ἀεὶ καὶ L   3. τοιοῦτος δὲ L

wind and generally the winds from that area bring rain
for those who dwell in the north.

5. It is not unimportant, nay, it is highly important
if the district has elevations.  For wherever the
clouds run into an obstacle and stop, rain is generated.  And so in adjoining districts different winds
are rainy in different areas.  But the rains have been
discussed elsewhere at length.  For the same reason the
north wind is forceful at its inception, while the south
wind is so as it ceases; hence the proverb about voyages
by sea.  The north wind hovers, as it were, directly
above those who live in the north, while the south wind
is far off.  The flow from far off takes more time and
happens when a mass has been accumulated.  For those
who live in Egypt and nearby the situation is reversed;
the south wind has force.  As a result, the proverb is
stated the other way around.

6. Thus, down there, the south wind is more frequent,
uniform, continuous, and regular.  For all winds are
like that for those who live nearby  (the place of
origin), but they are irregular and intermittent for
those who live at a distance.  These then must be
reckoned to be the causes of the above phenomena,
causes which are apparent also in other, smaller areas
and less distant from one another.  This may seem in-
correct, however, for the south wind is invariably fair
in places proper to it, while the north wind is cloudy

τοιοῦτος LAC. 4-14 LITT. CETT. δὲ τὰ πόρρω MSS. ⟨τοῖς⟩
MAR.VAS. τοῖς δὲ πόρρω SCHN. I E VERS. TURN.   4. μᾶλλον
DEIMPQ OM. CETT.,CAM.,FURL. 56   5. ἐκφανεῖς L ALD.,FURL.
56 ἐμφανεῖς CETT. τρόπους MSS. LOCIS  TURN. τόπους MAR.
VAS.,BON.  6. τοῦτο δ' οὖν καὶ δόξει 'ἂν ἄλογον MSS. τοῦ-
το δ' οὐκ 'ἂν δόξειεν ἀνάλογον SCHN. I τοῦτο δ' ἂν καὶ
δόξειεν ἄλογον εἶναι MAR.VAS.  7. ὁ μὲν γὰρ νότος τοῖς
FURL. 79   9. συνεφῆς ELOR ALD.

8

7.  αἴτιον δ' ὅτι διὰ μὲν τὸ μέγεθος πολὺν ἀέρα κινεῖ,
τοῦτον δὲ φθάνει ἐκπηγνὺς πρὶν ἀπῶσαι. παγέντα δὲ μένει τὰ
νέφη διὰ βάρος· εἰς ⟨δὲ⟩ τὰ ἔξω καὶ πορρωτέρω τὸ μέγεθος
μᾶλλον 'ἢ ἡ ψυχρότης διαδίδοται καὶ τοῦτο ἐργάζεται. ὁ δὲ
νότος ἧττόν τε ἔχων ὕλην, καὶ ταύτην οὐ πηγνὺς ἀλλ'ἀπωθῶν,
αἰθρίαν ἄγει τοῖς πλησίον, ὑετιώτερος δ'ἀεὶ τοῖς πόρρω μέγας πνέων καὶ λήγων μᾶλλον 'ἢ ἀρχόμενος, ὅτι ἀρχόμενος μὲν
ὀλίγον ἀέρα ἀπωθεῖται, προιὼν δὲ πλείω. καὶ οὕτως ἀθροιζό-
μενος ἐκνεφοῦταί τε καὶ πυκνωθεὶς ὑδάτιος γίνεται. ἔτι δὲ
καὶ τὸ ἀπ' ἐλάττονος 'ἢ μείζονος ἀρχῆς ἄρχεσθαι διαφέρει.
μικρᾶς γὰρ οὔσης αἴθριος, μεγάλης δ' ἐπινεφὴς καὶ ὑέτιος,
διὰ τὸ πλείω συνωθεῖν ἀέρα.

8.  τὸ δὲ μὴ πνεῖν κατ'αὐτὴν τὴν Αἴγυπτον ⟨τὰ⟩ πρὸς θάλατταν τὸν νότον, ὥς τινές φασι, μηδ' ὅσον ἡμέρας [ἀπέχοντα]
καὶ νυκτὸς δρόμον, ἀλλὰ τὰ ὑπὲρ Μέμφιδος λαμπρὸν, ὁμοίως
δὲ καὶ 'ἃ 'ἂν ἀπέχῃ τοσοῦτον, οὐκ ἀληθὲς μὲν εἶναί φασιν,
ἀλλὰ ψεῦδος. οὐ μὴν ἴσως γε, ἀλλ'ἔλαττον πνεῖ.τὸ δ'αἴτιον
ὅτι κοίλη τὰ κάτω ἡ Αἴγυπτος ὥσθ' ὑπερπίπτειν αὐτῆς· τὰ δ'
ἄνω ὑψηλότερα. ἐπεὶ τό γε σύνεγγυς ἀπαιτεῖ τὸ μέγεθος. τὰ
γὰρ τοιαῦτα μάλιστα ἐκ τῶν τόπων ἀποδοτέον, ἅπερ κατὰ φύσιν ἔχει. διαμένει δ' ἐπινεφῆ καὶ αἴθρια τὰ πνεύματα ταῦτα

---

7.  2. φθάνει ⟨ἡ ψυχρότης⟩ SCHN. IV 684  φθάνει καὶ πήγ-
νυσι MSS. ἐκπηγνὺς WI. εἰς ⟨δὲ⟩ EGO   3. ἔξω ⟨δὲ⟩ FURL. 57
τοῦ μεγέθους MSS. τὸ μέγεθος MAR.VAS.,FURL. 79 ἡ DI VAS.,
FURL. 79 'ἢ CETT. [ἡ ψυχρότης] SCHN. IV 684 'ἢ ἡ EGO   4.
καὶ τοῦτο ἐργαζομένη MSS.,SCHN. I καὶ τούτῳ ἐργάζεται
FURL. 79, SCHN. V,LVII καὶ τοῦτο ἐργάζεται WI.   5. ἀπαθῶν
BAS.   6. ὑέτιος BON.   7. μὲν ὅτι BAS.   8. οὕτως P VAS.,
FURL. 57 οὗτος CETT. τε OM. MU   9. ὑδάτινος MSS. ὑδάτιος
SCHN. I τὸ δὲ MSS. ἔτι δὲ καὶ τὸ SCHN. I

8.  1. κατὰ ταύτην τὴν MSS. κατ' αὐτὴν τὴν MAR.VAS.,BON.
⟨τὰ⟩ BON. ⟨τὴν⟩ FURL. 57 εἰς MSS. πρὸς SCHN. IV 684   2.
ἀπέχονται MSS. ἀπέχοντα FURL. 57 [ἀπέχοντα] STEINMETZ 29
4. ⟨'ἃ⟩ ἐὰν FURL. 57 'ἃ 'ἂν WI.  5. οὐ μὴν ἴσως γε ἀλλ'ἔλατ

in areas near (its origin), when there is a great storm, but cloudless in places farther away.

7. The reason is that because of its force it moves a mass of air and freezes this air before it can move it on; when the clouds freeze, they do not move because of their weight. It is the force rather than the coldness which is transmitted to distant places and there does its work. The south wind, having less material and not freezing it but moving it on, creates fair weather for the area nearby, but is always rainier in districts farther away. It blows with force when coming to an end rather than when beginning because at the beginning it moves little air, but moves more as it advances. The air thus collected becomes cloud and thus condensed becomes rainy. It also makes a difference that the wind begins from a smaller source, not a greater. If the source is small, the wind is fair; when the source is great, the wind is cloudy and rainy because it forces more air together.

8. The statement of some that the south wind does not blow at the coast of Egypt nor for a day and a night's travel from the shore, roughly speaking, while it is vigorous in the area above Memphis and likewise in places equally distant from the sea, is said to be false. But the fact is it does not blow as strongly but weaker. The reason is that Lower Egypt is sunken so that the wind bypasses it at a height. Upper Egypt is higher. Somehow or other, proximity (to the source) makes for force. Such phenomena are to be explained chiefly by reference to topography when they are in the

τὸν πνεῖ MSS. ἴσος TURN. ἐλάττων MAR.VAS. οὐ μὴν ἀλλ᾽ ἴσως γε ἔλαττον πνεῖ SCHN. II 589 πνεῖν BON. 8. καὶ φύσιν MSS κατὰ φύσιν WI. ἔχειν MSS. ἔχει SCHN. I ἅπερ...OM. FURL. 57 ταῦθ᾽ L ALD.,VAS. τοῦθ᾽ CETT. ταῦτα SCHN. I

ὁμοίως, ὥσπερ ἀρτίως ἐλέχθη.

9. τὸ δὲ τὸν βορέαν ἐπιπνεῖν τῷ νότῳ, τὸν δὲ νότον μὴ τῷ
βορέᾳ, πρὸς ἐκείνην τὴν αἰτίαν ἀνακτέον τὴν μερίζουσαν ἑκάτερα κατὰ τοὺς τόπους. παρ' ἡμῖν γὰρ τοῦτο συμβαίνει καὶ
ὅλως τοῖς ὑπὸ τὴν ἄρκτον οἰκοῦσιν, τοῖς δὲ πρὸς μεσημβρίαν
ἀνάπαλιν. αἴτιον δ' ἀμφοῖν τὸ αὐτό· τοῖς μὲν γὰρ ὁ βορέας,
τοῖς δ' ὁ νότος πλησίον· ὥστ' εὐθὺς ἀρχόμενοι ποιοῦσιν αἴσθησιν, εἰς δὲ τὰ πόρρω βραδέως διικνοῦνται.

10. πλείστων δ'ὄντων, ὥσπερ εἴρηται, βορείων καὶ νοτίων,
ἑκατέρων οἷον τάξις ⟨ἐστὶ⟩ ἐν οἷς χρόνοις μάλιστα πνέουσι
κατὰ λόγον [ἐστί].τοῖς μὲν βορείοις χειμῶνός τε καὶ θέρους
καὶ μετοπώρου μέχρι τοῦ λήγειν, τοῖς δὲ νοτίοις κατὰ χειμ-
ῶνά τε καὶ ἀρχομένου ⟨ἔαρος⟩ καὶ μετοπώρου λήγοντος. αὐταὶ
γὰρ αἱ τοῦ ἡλίου φοραὶ συνεργοῦσιν ἀμφοτέροις καὶ ἡ ἀνταπόδοσις γίνεται, καθάπερ παλιρροοῦντος τοῦ ἀέρος. ὃ γὰρ
⟨ἂν⟩ ἀπωσθῇ κατὰ χειμῶνα, (πλείους γὰρ ὡς ἐπίπαν βόρειοι
πνέουσι) καὶ ἔτι πρότερον τοῦ θέρους ὑπὸ τῶν ἐτησίων καὶ
τῶν ἐπὶ τούτοις, ἀνταποδίδοται πάλιν τοῦ ἦρος εἰς τούσδε
τοὺς τόπους, καὶ λήγοντος μετοπώρου καὶ περὶ πλειάδος δύ-
σιν ἀνάλογον.

11. ὅθεν καὶ τὸ θαυμαζόμενον ὡς οὐκ 'ὂν, διὰ τί βορέαι
μὲν ἐτησίαι γίνονται, νότοι δ' οὐ γίνονται, φαίνεταί πως
συμβαίνειν. οἱ γὰρ ἡρινοὶ νότοι καθάπερ ἐτησίαι τινές εἰσιν

---

9.   1. τὸ δὲ MSS. τὸ δὲ τὸ HEINS. τῷ νότῳ MSS. [τῷ] BAS.,
FURL. 57   2. 'ην μερ. MSS. τὴν TURN.,MAR.VAS. ἑκάτερον
FURL. 79   4. τοῦ δ' ἦρος πρὸς MSS. τοῖς δὲ πρὸς TURN.,
MAR.VAS.

10.   2. ἑκατέρας MSS. ἑκατέρων TURN.,MAR.VAS. ἑκατέροις
⟨συμβαίνει⟩ BON. τάξις τῶν χρόνων TURN. ⟨ἐστὶ⟩ EGO πνέουσι
LX₂Z ALD. πλέουσι CETT.   3. ἐστὶ DEIMOPQRUXZ [ἐστὶ] FURL.
57 [ἐστὶ...μετοπώρου] HEINS.   5. ⟨ἔαρος⟩ καὶ TURN.,MAR.
VAS. οὔτε γὰρ MSS. οὔτε αὐταὶ TURN.,MAR.VAS. καὶ γὰρ FURL.
57 E VERS. TURN. αὐταὶ γὰρ αἱ τοῦ ἡλίου EGO   7. ὁ γὰρ

order of nature. And these winds remain cloudy or fair in a way similar to that which we have just explained.

9. The fact that the north wind blows after the south wind, while the south wind does not follow the north wind, must be ascribed to its place. This is what happens in our land generally and in those to the north, but it is the reverse in the south. The reason is the same for both: the north wind is nearer to the former, the south wind to the latter, so that as soon as they get under way, they are perceptible, but they reach distant places more slowly.

10. The north winds and the south winds being the most frequent, as we have said, there is a certain orderliness about their periods. The north winds blow in the winter, in the summer, and in late autumn until the end of the season, while the south winds blow in winter, at the beginning of spring, and at the end of the late autumn. The motion of the sun itself contributes to both winds, and a reciprocating interchange takes place, with the air flowing back and forth, as it were. For what is dislodged in the winter (in general there are more north winds blowing) and earlier in the summer by the etesians and their successors, is restored to those places in the spring, at the end of late autumn, and at the setting of the Pleiades in proportion.

11. From this arises the puzzlement as to why there are northerly etesians but not southerly etesians, as though this were a fact; but it appears that there are southerly etesians. For the south winds in the spring

α.MSS. ὅταν γὰρ ἀπωσθῇ MAR.VAS. ὅταν ἀπωσθῇ ⟨ὁ ἥλιος⟩ BON. ʽὁ γὰρ ⟨ʼἀν⟩ ἀπωσθῇ SCHN. I

11.   1. FORTASSE ὡς ἄλογον SCHN. IV 686   3. χειμερινοὶ SALMASIUS 1260 ἐτησίαι LRUXZ ALD. κιτήσιοι CETT. ἐτησίαι

οὓς καλοῦσι λευκονότους· αἴθριοι γὰρ καὶ ἀσυννεφεῖς ὡς
ἐπίπαν ἅμα δὲ καὶ τῷ μακρὰν ἡμῶν ἀπηρτῆσθαι λανθάνουσιν.
ὁ δὲ βορέας εὐθὺς ἐν ἡμῖν. [ἥδε τῶν ἐτησίων φύσις] διὰ τί
δὲ ταύτην τὴν ὥραν καὶ τοσοῦτοι πνέουσι, καὶ διὰ τί λήγου-
σι τῆς ἡμέρας ληγούσης καὶ νύκτωρ οὐ πνέουσι, σχεδὸν ἐν
ταύταις λέγεται ταῖς αἰτίαις·ὡς ἄρα ἡ μὲν πνοὴ γίνεται διὰ
τὴν τῆς χιόνος τῆξιν. ὅταν μὲν οὖν ὁ ἥλιος ἄρξηται κρατεῖν
καὶ λύειν τὸν πάγον, οἱ πρόδρομοι,μετὰ δὲ ταῦτα οἱ ἐτησίαι.

12. τοῦ δὲ ἅμα τῇ καταφορᾷ τοῦ ἡλίου λήγειν καὶ νύκτωρ
μὴ πνεῖν αἴτιον τὸ τὴν χιόνα τηκομένην παύεσθαι δυομένου,
καὶ νύκτωρ μὴ τήκεσθαι δεδυκότος. οὐ μὴν ἀλλ' ἐνίοτε πνέουσιν, ὅταν πλείων ἡ τῆξις γένηται· καὶ γὰρ τῆς ἀνωμαλίας
αἴτιον τοῦτο ὑποληπτέον. ὁτὲ μὲν γαρ μεγάλοι καὶ συνεχεῖς,
ὁτὲ δ' ἐλάττους καὶ διαλείποντες πνέουσι διὰ τὸ τὰς τήξεις
ἀνωμαλεῖς γίνεσθαι. κατὰ δὲ τὴν ὕλην ἡ φορά. ταύτην δὲ τὴν
ἀνωμαλίαν ἐνδέχεται καὶ τοῖς τόποις καὶ τῷ σύνεγγυς 'ἢ
πόρρω καὶ ἄλλαις τοιαύταις διαφοραῖς συμβαίνειν.

13. εἰ δ' οὖν ἀληθὲς 'ὃ λέγουσιν ἄλλοι τε καὶ οἱ περὶ
Κρήτην, ὡς ἄρα νῦν μείζονες οἱ χειμῶνες καὶ χιὼν πλείων
πίπτει, τεκμήρια φέροντες ὡς τότε μὲν ᾠκεῖτο τὰ ὄρη, καὶ
ἔφερε καρπὸν καὶ τὸν σιτηρὸν καὶ τὸν δενδρίτην, πεφυτευμέ-

SCHN. I 4. ἀσυννεφεῖς MSS.,WI. ἀσυνεχεῖς SCHN. I 5. τὸ
μακρὸν ἡμῶν MSS. τῷ μακρὰν TURN.,MAR.VAS. μακραὶ SCHN. V,
LVII ἡμῶν DEL. SCHN. I, REST. II 589 λαμβάνουσιν MSS. λαν-
θάνουσιν MAR.VAS.,SCHN. I 6. ἥδε τῶν ἐτησίων φύσις MSS.,
DEL. WI. ὅθεν ἡ τῶν ἐτησίων φύσις SCHN. IV 686 E VERS.
FURL. 7. πῶς οὕτως MSS. τοσοῦτοι BON.,SCHN. I E PROB.
26,21 8. οὐ DEIMOPQRUXZ [οὐ] L ALD.,SCHN. I 10. τῆξιν
XZ SCHN. I πῆξιν CETT. 11. λύειν τὸν πάγον καὶ κρατεῖν
MSS.,SCHN. II 589 κρατεῖν καὶ λύειν τὸν πάγον SCHN. I

12. 3. δεδυκότος LZ ALD.,FURL. 58 δεδοικότος CETT. 4.
τῆξις LXZ ALD. πῆξις CETT. γίνηται MSS. γένηται SCHN. I

are etesians, those which are called white south winds;
they are fair-weather winds and cloudless on the whole.
At the same time, being remote from us, they are not no-
ticed. But the north wind is right at hand. Why they
blow at this season and in such strength; why they die
down when the day dies and do not blow at night, is explained more or less by the following causes: the breeze
occurs because of the melting of the snow; when the sun
begins to prevail and to dissolve the frost, there come
the "forerunners" and then the etesians.

12. The reason that these winds cease when the sun goes
down and do not blow at night is that as the sun is sinking, the snow ceases to melt, and at night, when the sun
has set, it no longer melts. Yet sometimes these winds
do blow (at night), when the melting is greater than
usual. This must be accounted the reason for the irregularity. Sometimes the winds blow strong and contin-
uously, sometimes weakly and intermittently, because of
the irregularity of the melting. The strength of the
wind is as the amount of material. This irregularity
can be ascribed to the lay of the land, the distance
near or far, and other such variations.

13. If it is true what the Cretans among others say,
that nowadays the winters are more severe and more snow
falls, adducing as evidence that the mountains were set-
tled in olden times and bore grain and fruit as the land

5. τοῦ LAC. 21 LITT. ληπτέον MSS. αἴτιον τοῦ ⟨τὸ ὑπο⟩λη-
πτέον. ὁτὲ μὲν γὰρ TURN.,MAR.VAS. μὲν γὰρ ὁτὲ μὲν μεγάλοι M ὁτὲ OM. CETT. πήξεις L 8. καὶ τὸ σύνεγγυς L καὶ τῷ
σύνεγγυς CETT.,SCHN. II 590 ἐκ τοῦ σύν. SCHN. I 9. συμβαίνειν LX₂Z ALD. συμβαίνει X₁CETT.

13. 1. τε OM. CAM. 3. ᾤκοιτο M ᾤκητο CETT. ᾠκεῖτο MAR.

νης καὶ διειργασμένης τῆς χώρας (ἔστι γὰρ πεδία ἐν τοῖς
Ἴδης ὄρεσιν εὐμεγέθη καὶ ἐν τοῖς ἄλλοις, ὧν νῦν οὐδ' ὁ-
τιοῦν γεωργοῦσι, διὰ τὸ μὴ φέρειν. τότε δ', ὥσπερ εἴρηται,
καὶ ἐπῴκουν· ὅθεν καὶ ἡ νῆσος πλήρης ἦν ἀνθρώπων, ὄμβρων
μὲν γενομένων κατ' ἐκεῖνον τὸν χρόνον πολλῶν, χιόνων δὲ
καὶ χειμώνων μὴ γινομένων), εἰ δ'ἔστιν ἀληθῆ ταῦτα, καθάπερ λέγομεν, ἀναγκαῖον καὶ τοὺς ἐτησίας εἶναι πλείους.

14.  εἰ δέ ποτ' ἐξέλιπον καὶ Ἀρισταῖος αὐτοὺς ἀνεκαλέσ-
ατο θύσας τὰς ἐν Κέῳ θυσίας τῷ Διί, καθάπερ μυθολογοῦσι,
κάτομβρα [μὲν] 'ἂν εἴη τὰ ἐπιχειμέρια οὐχ ὁμοίως οὐδὲ χιο-
νώδη. ταῦτα δ' εἴ τινα ἔχει διαλλαγὴν εἴτε τεταγμένην εἴτ'
ἄτακτον, εἴη 'ἂν καὶ τῶν πνευμάτων παῦλα καὶ μεταλλαγὴ κατὰ τοὺς αὐτοὺς χρόνους. ἄτοπον δ' 'ἂν δόξειεν, εἰ μὴ καὶ
τοῖς πρὸς μεσημβρίαν ἐστὶ τοιαύτη τις ἐπικουρία κατὰ τὸ
ἔτος· πολλῷ γὰρ ἐμπυρώτερος ὁ τόπος ἐκεῖνος. δῆλον οὖν τοῦτο, πλὴν ⟨ὅτι οἱ μὲν ὑστερίζουσι⟩ τῶν καρπῶν, οἱ δὲ προτε-
ροῦσιν, οἱ δ' ἀπαθεῖς. περὶ μὲν [οὖν] τούτων σκεπτέον.

15.  εἰ δὲ πάντων τῶν πνευμάτων ἡ αὐτὴ καὶ ὑπὸ τῶν αὐτῶν
γένεσις (τῷ τι παραλαβεῖν), ὁ ἥλιος 'ἂν ὁ ποιῶν εἴη. τάχα
δ' οὐκ ἀληθές, καθόλου εἰπεῖν, ἀλλ' ὡς ἡ ἀναθυμίασις, οὐ-

VAS. ὄρη. ἔφερε HEINS. σίδηρον MSS. σίτηρον MAR.VAS.  6.
ἴδης LX₂Z ALD. ἴδοις M ἰδίοις X₁CETT. ἰδαίοις SCHN. V,LVII
9. πολλῶν δὲ χρόνων M₁ πολλῶν χρόνων M₂CETT. πολλῶν, χιόνων MAR.VAS.,BON.    10. εἰ δ' MSS. εἰ δὴ SCHN. IV 687 ὅπερ
λέγομεν U καθάπερ λέγ. CETT. καθ' λέγεται SCHN. IV 687
ὅπερ λέγουσιν WI.

14.  1. ἐξέλιπον R₂ SCHN. I ἐξέλειπον R₁CETT.  3. [μὲν]
'ἂν LX₂ ALD.,FURL. 58 μὲν 'ἂν CETT. δεῖ MSS. δ' εἰ MAR.
VAS.,BON. ἔχειν MSS. ἔχει BON.,SCHN. I τεταγμένη OPQRUXZ
τεταγμένην EILMO   5. ⟨οὖν⟩ 'ἂν FURL. 59  6. καὶ τοὺς X₁
κατὰ τοὺς X₂CETT. καὶ τοῖς SCHN. I  7. ἔστι MSS. FORT.
εἴη SCHN. II 590 τὴν τοιαύτη τις CAM. ἦθος MSS. ἔτος MAR.
VAS. πόρρω X₁ πολλῷ X₂CETT. ἐκπυρώτερος MSS. ἐμπυρώτερος
SCHN. II 590 ἐνπυρώσεως SCHN. V,LVII πλὴν εἴη μιση τὸν

was planted and tilled (for there are extensive plains
among the mountains of Ida and in the other mountains,
none of which are worked now because of infertility.
Whereas in those days, as we have said, they were set-
tled, as a result of which the island was populous,
because then the rains were generous, while snowfalls
and wintry weather did not often occur), if then what
they say is true, the etesian winds must be more numerous (today).

14. If the etesians ever failed and Aristaeus recalled
them, according to the myth, by sacrificing to Zeus on
Ceos, the exposed territories were not as subjected to
rain and snow. If these areas undergo any variation
whether orderly or irregular, there will be a stoppage
and a change of the winds at those times. It would seem
illogical if there is not some such annual relief for
those who live in the south, for it is much hotter there.
This much is clear, except that some crops mature earlier, some later, some are unaffected. This subject must
be investigated.

15. If the generation of all winds is the same and
caused by the same factors (by taking on some material),
the sun is the agent. Perhaps this is not correct taken
universally, but rather the exhalation is the cause,

---

καρπὸν U₂ πλὴν ἑις LAC. 15 LITT. εἱς μιση U₁CETT.,ALD.
πλὴν εἰ μὴ ὥσπερ οἱ μὲν ὑστεροῦσι τῶν καρπῶν TURN.,MAR.
VAS. δῆλον οὖν τοῦτο, ὅτι τῶν μὲν καρπῶν BON. πάλιν διὰ
τί ἔνιοι τῶν καρπῶν ὀψίζουσι, οἱ δὲ προτερίζουσι BON.,E
VERS. TURN. πλὴν ⟨ὅτι οἱ μὲν ὑστερίζουσι⟩ τῶν καρπῶν, οἱ
δὲ EGO    10. ⟨οὖν⟩ SCHN. I

15.    1. εἰ δὲ L ALD.,FURL. 59 αἱ δὲ CETT. αἱ αὐταὶ Z    2.
τι OM. EOR πα LAC. βεῖν EIMOU παραλαβεῖν CETT. τῷ δὲ παραλαβεῖν SC. πνεῦμα γίνεσθαι BON. ὁ EOR OM. CETT. ἄνω ποιῶν

τος δ' ὡς συνεργῶν. ἀλλ' ὁ ἥλιος δοκεῖ καὶ κινεῖν ἀνατέλλων καὶ καταπαύειν τὰ πνεύματα· διὸ καὶ ἐπαυξάνεται καὶ
πίπτει πολλάκις. οὐ καθόλου δὲ τοῦτ' ἀληθές,ἀλλ'ἐφ'ὧν γε
συμβαίνει, ταύτην ὑποληπτέον τὴν αἰτίαν. ὅταν μὲν γὰρ ἔ-
λαττον ᾖ τὸ ἀνηγμένον ὑγρόν, τούτου κατακρατῶν ἐξανήλωσε
καὶ κατέπαυσεν ὁ ἥλιος· ὅταν δὲ πλέον, συμπαρώρμησε καὶ
σφοδροτέραν ἐποίησε τὴν κίνησιν.

16. ἐνίοτε δὲ καὶ ἅμα τῇ δύσει κατέπαυσεν, ὥσπερ ἀφελό-
μενος τὴν ἀπ' αὐτοῦ κίνησιν ῾ἣν ἔδωκεν. ταύτην δὲ δῆλον
ὡς ἔχειν τινὰ δεῖ συμμετρίαν, ὥστε μήτε ἐξαναλίσκεσθαι
μήτ' ἐξ αὐτῆς δύνασθαι κινεῖσθαι πλείω χρόνον. ἔνια δὲ καὶ
δύνοντος τοῦ ἡλίου πνεῖν οὐδὲν κωλύει μᾶλλον,οἷον ὅσα κα-
τέχεται τῇ θερμότητι, καὶ ὥσπερ ἀναξηραίνεται καὶ ἐκκαίεται. διὰ τοῦτο γὰρ καὶ ἐν μεσημβρίᾳ μάλιστα ἀπνεύματοι·
παρεγκλίναντος δὲ τοῦ ἡλίου πνευματωδέστεραι.

17. ποιεῖ δὲ καὶ ἡ σελήνη ταῦτα πλὴν οὐχ ὁμοίως· οἷον
γὰρ ἀσθενὴς ἥλιός ἐστι. διὸ καὶ νύκτωρ δεινότεραι ⟨αἱ πνο-
αὶ⟩, καὶ αἱ σύνοδοι τῶν μηνῶν χειμερινώτεραι. συμβαίνει δ'
οὖν ὁτὲ μὲν ἀνατέλλοντος τοῦ ἡλίου τὰ πνεύματα ἐπαίρεσθαι,
ὁτὲ δὲ λήγειν. καὶ ἐπὶ τῆς δύσεως ὁμοίως· ὁτὲ μὲν γὰρ κατέπαυσεν, ὁτὲ δὲ ὥσπερ ἀφῆκεν. εἰ δέ ποτε καὶ κατὰ σύμπτωμα
γίνοιτο ταῦτα, καθάπερ καὶ τὰ ἐπὶ τῶν ἄστρων ἀνατολαῖς
καὶ δύσεσιν, ἐπισκεπτέον. [ταὐτὸ δὲ]

MSS. ᾿ἀν ὁ ποιῶν TURN.,MAR.VAS. 3. οὕτως MSS. οὗτος BON.
E VERS. TURN.,SCHN. I 4. ὁ συνεργῶν U καὶ κινεῖν MSS. δὲ
κινεῖν FURL. 59 6. ἐμπίπτει DLXZ ALD. καὶ πίπτει CETT.,
TURN.,SCHN. I 8. ἐξανήλωκε MSS. ἐξανήλωσε SCHN. I

16. 1. κατέπαυσεν IQX₂Z ALD.,FURL. 59 6. ἐξαναξηραίνε-
ται DLXZ ALD.,SCHN. I ἀναξηραίνεται CETT.,SCHN. V 160 ἐγ-
καίεται MSS. ἐκκαίεται SCHN. II 590 7. πνεύματα L ALD.
ἀπνεύματοι CETT. ἀναπνεύματα TURN. ἄπνευματα MAR.VAS.,BON.
πνεύματα παύονται FURL. 84 8. SC. πνοαὶ WOOD-SYMONS

17. 1. ταῦτα MSS. ταὐτὰ SCHN. I E VERS. TURN. 2.δεινό-

while the sun assists. But the sun by rising seems both to set the winds in motion and to halt them. Therefore the winds augment and die down frequently. This statement is not universally true, but the following must be considered the cause when the increase and lapse take place: when the moisture raised is modest in amount, the sun overcomes it, uses it up, and causes it to cease, whereas when it is in greater amount, the sun adds a stronger and more active motion.

16. Sometimes the sun, by removing the motion, as it were, which it has imparted, halts the wind when it sets. Plainly, the motion must have some proportion so that the wind is not consumed nor kept moving an overlong time. Nothing prevents some winds from blowing more strongly when the sun goes down, such as those which are repressed by the heat and, as it were, dried up and burned out. For this reason these winds are quiet at midday generally and gain strength when the sun is sinking.

17. The moon has this effect also, but not to the same degree, being a kind of weak sun. Therefore the breezes are more powerful at night and the weather stormier at the full moon. And so, when the sun is rising, the winds now rise, now abate. It is the same with the setting sun; sometimes it halts the winds, sometimes it lets loose. The question whether these things happen in conjunction, as at the risings and settings of the stars, must be looked into.

τεραι LAC. 17 LITT. MSS. δεινότεραι αἱ ἐκλείψεις TURN., MAR.VAS. E METEOR. II 8 διὸ καὶ νύκτες εὐδιεινότεραι ἐν ταῖς πανσελήναις BON. δεινότερα FORT. δυνατώτερα FURL. 85 ⟨αἱ πνοαὶ⟩ EGO 3. χειμερινωτέρους FURL. 85 7. [τὰ] FURL. 85 τὰ κατὰ ἐπὶ HEINS. 8. ἐπισπεπτέον ταὐτὸ δὲ καὶ MSS. ἐπισκεπτέον τοῦτο SCHN. IV 688 ἐπισκεπτέον τοῦτ' ' ἂν εἴη WI. ταὐτὸ δὲ DELEO

18.   καὶ ἀπὸ τῆς αὐτῆς πως αἰτίας καὶ διὰ μέσων νυκτῶν
καὶ μεσημβρίας ἄπνοιαι γίνονται [καὶ] μάλιστα. συμβαίνει
γὰρ ποτὲ μὲν κρατεῖν, ποτὲ δὲ κρατεῖσθαι τὸν ἀέρα τὸν τοιοῦτον ὑπὸ τῶν ⟨τοῦ ἡλίου ἀκτίνων⟩· μέσων μὲν νυκτῶν κρατ-
εῖν· πορρωτάτω γὰρ ὁ ἥλιος τότε. μεσημβρίας [δὲ κρατεῖν
ποτὲ] δὲ κρατεῖσθαι [τὸν ἀέρα τὸν τοιοῦτον]. κρατῶν δὲ καὶ
κρατούμενος ἕστηκεν. ἡ δὲ στάσις νηνεμία. συμβαίνει δὲ καὶ
τὰς καταπαύσεις γίνεσθαι τῶν κατὰ λόγον· ἄρχεται μὲν γὰρ 'ἡ
περὶ ἕω 'ἡ περὶ δυσμάς. λήγει δὲ τὰ μὲν ἕωθεν ὅταν κρατη-
θῇ· κρατεῖται δὲ κατὰ μεσημβρίαν· τὰ δ' ἀπὸ δυσμῶν, ὅταν
παύσηται κρατῶν. τοῦτο δὲ γίνεται μέσων νυκτῶν.

19.   εἰ δέ τινες θαυμάζουσιν ὡς ἄλογον, ὅτι τὰ πνεύματα
ψυχρά ἐστιν ἀπὸ τῆς τοῦ ἡλίου κινήσεως καὶ ἁπλῶς τοῦ θερμοῦ γινόμενα, ψεῦδος τὸ φαινόμενον αὐτοῖς ἄλογον· οὔτε γὰρ
ἁπλῶς ἀλλ' ὡς συναιτίῳ προσαπτέον, οὔτε πάντως ἡ ὑπὸ θερμο-
οῦ κίνησις θερμὴ καὶ πυρώδης, ἀλλ' ἐὰν τρόπον τινὰ γίνηται.
ἀθρόως μὲν γὰρ ἐμπίπτουσα καὶ [ἡ] συνεχὴς αὐτῷ τῷ ἀφιέντι
θερμή. κατὰ μικρὸν δὲ καὶ διὰ στενοῦ τινος, αὐτὴ μὲν θερμή,
ὁ δ' ὑπὸ ταύτης κινούμενος ἀήρ, ὁποῖος  ἄν ποτε τυγχάνῃ

---

18.   1. ἐπὶ MSS. ἀπὸ SCHN. I [ῶς] WI. διὰ τί μέσων νυκτῶν
SCHN. IV 689 E VERS. TURN. ταὐτὸ δὲ καὶ ἐπὶ τῆς νηνεμίας
FURL. 85   2. [καὶ] SCHN. I   2-7. συμβαίνει γάρ ποτε μὲν
κρατεῖν, ποτὲ δὲ (καὶ L) κρατεῖσθαι τὸν ἀέρα τοιοῦτον ὑπὸ
τῶν LAC. 17 LITT. (SINE LAC. L) μέσων μὲν νυκτῶν κρατεῖν
πορρωτάτω γὰρ ὅ ἥλιος τότε μεσημβρίας δὲ κρατεῖν ποτὲ δὲ
κρατεῖσθαι τὸν ἀέρα τὸν τοιοῦτον, κρατῶν δὲ κρατούμενος
ἕστηκεν (δὲ κρατεῖν...τοιοῦτον OM. L ALD.) MSS.   4. ὑπ'
αὐτῶν MAR.VAS.   4-6. μέσων μὲν νυκτῶν κρατεῖν· πορρωτάτω
γὰρ ὁ ἥλιος τότε...μεσημβρίας. κρατῶν δὲ καὶ κτλ. SCHN. I
συμβαίνει γὰρ τὸ τοιοῦτον ὥστε ποτὲ μὲν κρατεῖν, ποτὲ δὲ
κρατεῖσθαι τὸν ἀέρα ὑπὸ τῶν ἀκτίνων. καὶ μέσων νυκτῶν κρατεῖ πορρωτάτω SCHN. IV 689 τοιοῦτον ὑπὸ τοῦ ἡλίου. καὶ
μέσων νυκτῶν πορρωτάτω WI. ὑπὸ τῶν ⟨τοῦ ἡλίου ἀκ-

18. The winds become still, as a general rule, around
midnight and midday from the same cause. The air of
that kind is at the one time overcoming and at another
time overcome by the rays of the sun. The air prevails
at midnight, for the sun is farthest away; at midday it
is being overcome. Both when prevailing and when being
overcome, the air comes to a standstill. This is a calm.
The stoppages come about also in a systematic way. The
winds begin at dawn or sunset. Some winds die down
starting at dawn, when they are being overcome, and they
are overcome by midday. Others die down starting at sundown, when the sun ceases to prevail. The calm comes at
midnight.

19. If some thinkers find it strange and illogical that
the winds which are brought about by the motion of the
sun and of heat generally are themselves cold, they are
mistaken as to the illogicality. The effect must not be
attributed to the sun alone but only as an aid, nor is
the motion caused by the heat hot and fiery universally
but only when caused in a certain way. The motion is
hot when coming compactly and in connection with the im-
pelling agent; when issuing in small amounts and advanc-
ing through a narrow passage, the motion is itself hot,
but the air which it sets in motion produces a motion

---

τίνων⟩ EGO   5. μεσημβρίας DEL. BON. VEL SCRIBENDUM μεσημβρίας δὲ κρατεῖσθαι, ἐγγυτάτω γὰρ γίνεται. τότε ὑπ' αὐτῶν
μέσων BON. μεσημβρίας δὲ κρατεῖται WI. ⟨κρατεῖσθαι δὲ⟩ μεσημβρίας EGO   8. γενέσθαι MSS. γίνεσθαι SCHN. I ἄρχεται
γὰρ ἡ θερμὴ περὶ δυσμὰς MSS. ἄρχεται ⟨μὲν⟩ 'ἡ περὶ ἔω 'ἡ
περὶ δυσμὰς MAR.VAS.,BON.   10. κατὰ μεσημβρίαν καὶ ἀπὸ
δυσμῶν MSS. μεσημβρίαν δὲ καὶ τὸ ἀπὸ δυσμῶν BON. ⟨τὰ δὲ⟩
SCHN. I   11. κρατῶν MSS. κρατοῦντα MAR.VAS.,FURL. 59

19.   4. ἄλλως MSS. ἀλλ' ὡς FURL. 60 ἢ ἀπὸ FURL. 86   5.
γίνεται L ALD.,FURL. 60 γίνηται CETT.   6. μὲν γὰρ ἐκπίπτ.

προυπάρχων, τοιαύτην καὶ τὴν κίνησιν ἀποδίδωσιν.

20. παραδεῖγμα δὲ ἱκανὸν τὸ ἐκ τῶν στομάτων ἀφιέμονον, ὅ
φασιν εἶναι θερμὸν καὶ ψυχρὸν, οὐκ ἀληθῆ λέγοντες.ἀλλ'ἀεὶ
μὲν θερμόν ἐστι ⟨τὸ ἐξιὸν⟩, διαφέρει δὲ τῇ προέσει καὶ ἐκ-
πτώσει. χανόντων μὲν γὰρ καὶ ἀθρόον ἀφιέντων θερμόν. ἐὰν
δὲ διὰ στενοῦ σφοδρότερον φερόμενον ὠθῇ τὸν πλησίον ἀέρα.
κἀκεῖνος τὸν ἐχόμενον ψυχρὸν ὄντα,καὶ ἡ πνοὴ καὶ ἡ κίνησις
γίνεται ψυχρά. τὸ αὐτὸ δὲ καὶ ἐπὶ τῶν πνευμάτων συμβαίνει·
διὰ στενοῦ γὰρ ἰούσης τῆς πρώτης κινήσεως,αὐτὸ μὲν τὸ πρῶτον οὐ ψυχρόν·τὸ δὲ ὑπὸ τούτου κινούμενον, ὡς 'ἀν ἔχον
τυγχάνῃ πρὸς θερμότητα καὶ ψυχρότητα. ψυχροῦ μὲν [γὰρ]
ὄντος, ψυχρὸν, θερμοῦ δὲ, θερμόν. καὶ διὰ τοῦτο θέρους μὲν
θερμὰ, χειμῶνος δὲ ψυχρὰ ⟨τὰ⟩ πνεύματα. καθ' ἑκατέραν γὰρ
τὴν ὥραν τοιοῦτος ὁ ἀήρ.

21. φανερὸν δ' ὅπου διὰ τὴν ⟨θερμότητα ὁ τόπος⟩ ἐκπυρωμέν-
νον ἀέρα τετύχηκεν. ἐὰν γὰρ ὅπου ⟨πνεῖ τὸ⟩ πνεῦμα καὶ ὁ
τόπος ⟨ἔμπυρος ἢ εἴτε⟩ θερμὸν εἴτε ψυχρὸν, ὅμως...⟨ἡ⟩ διαφορὰ τοῦ ἀέρος ὁποῖος 'ἀν ᾖ τοιοῦτος φαίνεται. καὶ ἐν αὐτοῖς μὲν τοῖς τόποις καὶ τοῖς συνεχέσιν ἔμπυρος ἡ πνοὴ

MSS. ἐμπίπτουσα BON. μὲν OM. FURL. 60 REST. SCHN. II 590,
WI. ἡ συνεχὴς MSS. καὶ εἰ σύνεγγυς BON. ἡ OM. FURL. 60  8.
ὁ δ' ὑπὸ MSS.ἀὴρ δ' ὑπὸ MAR.VAS. κινούμενος αὐτὸ MSS.
κιν. ἀὴρ BON.,FURL. 60 E PROB. 26,48    9. πρόσω ὑπάρχων
MSS. προυπάρχων MAR.VAS.,BON. τοιαύτην δὲ MSS. τοι. καὶ
BON.,FURL. 60

20. 3. ⟨τὸ ἐξιὸν⟩ SCHN. I E PROB. 26,48    4. χαινόντων
MSS. χανόντων SCHN. I    5. ὠθῇ FURL. 60    6. ψυχρῶν ὄντων MSS. ψυχρὸν ὄντα BON.,FURL. 60 ψυχροῦ δὲ ὄντος τοῦ
ἀέρος SCHN. II 591    8. οὔσης MSS. ἰούσης STEIN. 39    9.
ἔχον MSS. ἔχειν CAM. 10. μὲν γὰρ MSS. [γὰρ] MAR.VAS.,
SCHN. I    12. ⟨τὰ⟩ πν. BON.,SCHN. II 591

21. 1. διὰ τὴν LAC. 16 LITT. ἐκπεπυρωμένον οἷον τετύχηκεν MSS. διὰ τὴν ⟨θερμὴν VEL αὐτὴν⟩ MAR.VAS. διὰ τὴν ⟨θερ-

which is of whatever temperature the air was previously.

20. A good example of this is the breath we release from our mouths, which is said to be hot and cold, mistakenly, since it is always hot but differs in the way it is projected. When we release it mouth agape and in a body, it is warm, but when it is released through pursed lips vigorously, it impels the nearby air and this air the next, which is cold, and so the breath and the motion are cold. This same thing happens with the winds. When the first motion passes through a constriction, the wind is at first not cold, but the matter set in motion by it is hot or cold according to its condition when encountered. If it was cold, it remains cold; if it was hot, it remains hot. For this reason winds are hot in summer and cold in winter. For the air is in keeping with the season.

21. This is clear wherever the district has torrid air because of the heat. For if the district is superheated where the wind blows, be it hot or cold, yet . . . whatever the temperature of the air is is revealed by the difference (in the winds). In these districts and those ad-

---

μότητα ὁ τόπος⟩ ἐκπεπυρωμένον ἀέρα τετύχηκεν BON.    2. ἐὰν γὰρ ὅπου LAC. 16 LITT. καὶ ὁ πόθος LAC. 14 LITT. θερμὸν εἴτε ψυχρὸν MSS. πνεῦμα καὶ ὁπότε MAR.VAS. ἐὰν γὰρ ὅπου ῥεῖ τὸ πνεῦμα καὶ ὁ τόπος ἐνταῦθα ἔμπυρος ᾖ εἴτε θερμὸν εἴτε ψυχρόν, ὅμως καὶ πρὸς τῇ διαφορᾷ τοῦ ἀέρος ἀεὶ τοιοῦτον BON. διὰ τὴν ἀναθυμίασιν οἷον ἐκπεπυρωμένος τόπος. ἐὰν γὰρ ὅπου τὸ πνεῦμα ὁποιονοῦν εἴτε θερμὸν εἴτε ψυχρὸν ὅμως ἡ διαφορά SCHN. IV 692 E VERS. TURN.    3. ὅμως LAC. 20 LITT. διαφορὰ τοῦ ἀέρος LAC. 18 LITT. 'ἂν ᾖ τοιοῦτος φαίνεται καὶ ἐν αὐτοῖς μὲν τοῖς τόποις 16 LITT. τοῖς συνεχέσιν MSS. τοῦ ἀέρος η οπο LAC. P ἀέρος ὁποῖος 'ἂν ᾖ SCHN. V,LVII    4. ⟨καὶ⟩ τοῖς συνεχέσιν MAR.VAS.,SCHN. I    8. πα-

γίνεται, πορρωτέρω δὲ προιοῦσιν οὐχ ὁμοίως. ἐνίοτε δὲ καὶ
τὸ ἄλλοθεν ἐπιὸν, ἐὰν ἐξ ἐμπύρων ᾖ τόπων καὶ ἐχόντων ἀέρα
παχὺν καὶ διακεκαυμένον, ὑπερβάλλον φαίνεται τῇ θερμότητι.
διὸ καὶ οἱ ὁδοπόροι [μὲν] καὶ θερισταὶ πολλάκις ἀποθνήσ-
κουσιν ὑπὸ τῶν τοιούτων πνευμάτων ἐν τοῖς πεδίοις καὶ ἐν
τοῖς πνιγηροῖς τόποις, τὰ μὲν αὐτοῦ συνεργαζομένου τοῦ
προυπάρχοντος ἀέρος, τὰ δὲ τοῦ διαφόρου, διὰ τὴν πνοὴν
καὶ τὴν πρόσπτωσιν.

22. ...ὅτι γε οὔτ' αὐτὸς ὑφ' αὐτοῦ μόνον κινούμενος ὁ ἀὴρ
οὔθ' ὑπὸ τοῦ θερμοῦ κρατούμενος ταύτην φέρεται τὴν φοράν,
κἀκεῖθεν δῆλον· εἰ μὲν γὰρ ὑφ' αὐτοῦ διὰ τὸ ψυχρὸς εἶναι φύσει καὶ ἀτμιδώδης, κάτω 'ἂν ἐφέρετο· εἰ δ' ὑπὸ τοῦ θερμοῦ,
ἄνω. τοῦ γὰρ πυρὸς κατὰ φύσιν αὕτη ἡ φορά. νῦν δ' ὥσπερ ἐξ
ἀμφοῖν μικτὴ, διὰ τὸ μηδ' ἕτερον κρατεῖν.

23. τούτῳ μὲν οὖν καθόλου τῷ κοινῷ, ὅτι ὁποῖος 'ἂν ὁ ἀὴρ
'ἢ ἡ ἀναθυμίασις καθ' ἑκάστους ᾖ τόπους, οὕτως ἕξει καὶ
τὰ πνεύματα τῇ ψυχρότητι, καὶ τάδε συμμαρτυρεῖ· ὅσα γὰρ ἀπὸ
ποταμῶν 'ἢ λιμνῶν, πάντα ψυχρά, διὰ τὴν ψυχρότητα τοῦ ἀέρος. ἀποψύχεται [μὲν] γὰρ ἀπολείποντος τοῦ ἡλίου, καὶ ἅμα
παχύτερος ὁ ἀτμὸς, καὶ ἔτι ⟨μᾶλλον⟩ δ' εἰ σύνεγγυς. ὥσθ'
ὅταν προσπίπτῃ, συμβαίνει καθάπερ ῥίγωσίν τινα γίνεσθαι

χὺν CAM διακείμενον MSS. διακαῇ FURL. 60 FORT. διακεκαυμένον SCHN. V 160,WI.   9. μὲν MSS. [μὲν] SCHN. I   11.
πνιγεροῖς MSS. πνιγηροῖς MAR.VAS.,BON τὰ μὲν MSS. τὸ μὲν
BON.,FURL. 60 συνυπάρχοντος MSS. προυπάρχοντος SCHN. IV
692   12. τὸ δὲ MSS. τὰ δὲ SCHN. I

22.   1. ὅπου δ' ὑπ' αὐτοῦ μόνος MSS. ὅτι οὔτ' ὑφ' αὐτοῦ
TURN. ὅτι δ' ὑφ' αὐτοῦ MAR.VAS. ὅτι δ' ὑπ' αὐτοῦ μόνος
FURL. 60 ὅτι δὲ οὔτ' αὐτὸς ὑπ' αὐτοῦ μόνος FURL. 86 ὅτι γε
EGO E PROB. 26,48 μόνον SCHN. I ὁ ἀὴρ ὁ ὑπὸ θερμοῦ MSS. ὁ
ἀὴρ οὔτ' ὑπὸ BON. οὔθ' SCHN. I   2. φέρεται MSS. φαίνεται
VAS.   3. ⟨ὑφ' αὐτοῦ⟩ MAR.VAS.,SCHN. I ψύχος MSS. ψυχρὸς
BON.,FURL. 60 φύσει εἶναι EOPQRUXZ εἶναι OM. CETT. ALD.
εἶναι φύσει SCHN. I   4. εἶτα D εἶπε $Z_1$ εἶθ' $LZ_2$ ALD.

joining, the wind is superheated, but as we proceed, not to the same degree. Sometimes a breeze coming from a hot climate and having thick and burnt-out air is seen to be excessively hot. Thus travelers and reapers in the fields in stifling hot areas are often killed by such winds, in part because the air already present contributes its effect, in part because the other air has an effect, brought in by the wind.

22. . . . That the air is not self-moving nor takes this direction because overcome by heat is clear from the following: if air were self-moving, being cold and vaporous by nature, it would move downwards; if it were moved by heat, it would move upwards. For the motion of fire is naturally upwards. In fact, the motion is in a sense a compound of both because neither prevails.

23. And this general principle that the winds will have the same temperature as the air or the exhalation has in any given place is supported by the following: all winds emanating from rivers and lakes are cold because of the moisture of the air. When the sun fails, the vapor is cooled and at the same time condensed, and all the more if in the immediate vicinity, with the result that when

εἴτ' CETT. εἰ δὲ TURN.   5. τὸ γὰρ πῦρ ὡς κατὰ MSS. τοῦ γὰρ πυρὸς κατὰ MAR.VAS.,BON. E VERS. TURN.

23.   1. τοῦτο μὲν οὖν καθόλου τὸ κοινὸν MSS. τούτῳ...τῷ κοινῷ SCHN. I ἢ VEL 'ἡ MSS. ⟨ἡ⟩ SCHN. I   2. τὰ πνεύματα τῇ θερμότητι καὶ τῇ ψυχρότητι STEIN. 44   3. ὅσα γε   4. ὑγρότητα MSS. ψυχρότητα BON.   5. ἀποψύχεται LZ FURL. 61 ἀποψύχηται CETT. μὲν OM. WI.   6. ἡ σύνεγγυς MSS. εἰ σύν. BON.,SCHN. I ἢ σύν. FURL. 87 καὶ ἔτι ⟨μᾶλλον⟩ δ' εἰ SCHN. V,LVII,WI.   7. συμπίπτει Z₁ συμπίπτη Z₂ προσπίπτει EO CAM. προσπίπτη CETT. ῥᾶσιν MSS. ῥῶσιν FURL. 61,SCHN. I ῥίγωσιν WI. γίνεσθαι DEIL SCHN. I γενέσθαι CETT.

τοῖς σώμασι.

24. καὶ διὰ τοῦτο πολλάκις ἔγκοιλοι καὶ ἐπισκεπεῖς τινες
ὄντες τόποι πρὸς τὰ ἔξω πνεύματα ὑπὸ τῶν ἐγχωρίων εἰσι ψυ-
χροί· τὸ γὰρ ἀναχθὲν ὑπὸ τοῦ ἡλίου μένειν οὔτε πεφυκὸς οὔτε δυνάμενον φέρεται καὶ ποιεῖ πνοήν. ὅθεν αἵ τε ἀπὸ τῶν
ποταμῶν καὶ λιμνῶν αὖραι καὶ ὅλως αἱ ἀπόγειαι πνέουσιν ἕωθεν,ἀποψυχομένης τῆς ἀτμίδος διὰ τὴν ἀπόλειψιν τοῦ θερμοῦ.
τὴν γὰρ αὖραν τοιαύτην γίνεσθαι κατὰ λόγον ἐστὶ διά τε
τἆλλα καὶ διὰ τὴν εὐδίαν· καὶ ὅταν ψεκάδια καὶ ὑετοὶ μέτριοι γίνωνται, μᾶλλον πνέουσι. προσγίνεται γὰρ ὕλη τότε
πανταχοῦ, καὶ μᾶλλον αἱ ἀπόγειαι γίνονται μετὰ τοῦτο.

25. ἀπὸ μόνου δὲ τοῦ Νείλου δοκοῦσιν οὐκ ἀποπνεῖν αὖραι
'ἢ ἐλάχισται, διότι θερμὸς ὁ τόπος καὶ ἐξ οὗ καὶ εἰς 'ὸν
ῥεῖ· αἱ δ' αὖραι πυκνουμένου τοῦ ὑγροῦ εἰσι. διὸ καὶ οὐδ'
ἀπὸ τῶν ἐν Λιβύῃ ποταμῶν οὐδ' ἀφ' ἑνὸς αὖραι οὐδαμῶς·ἅπαν-
τες γὰρ θερμοί. τοῦτο δὲ δῆλον, ὅτι ἀπὸ τῶν περὶ Βαβυλῶνα
καὶ Σοῦσα, καὶ ὅλως πρὸς τοὺς ἐμπύρους τόπους. καίτοι φασί
γε θαυμαστῶς καταψύχεσθαι τὸν ἀέρα πρὸς τὴν ἕω. τοῦτο μὲν
οὖν ἐπισκεπτέον. τάχα γὰρ ἀποψύχεται μέν, οὐ δύναται δὲ
πορρωτέρω προιέναι, καὶ ποιεῖν αὖραν,ἐμπύρων εὐθὺ τῶν ὑπο-
δεχομένων ὄντων τόπων.

---

24. 1. εὐσκεπεῖς MSS. ἐπισκεπεῖς SCHN. IV 693   2. πρὸς
τὰ ἔξω πνεύματα MAR.VAS.   3. οὐδὲ ΕΙΜΟPQR οὔτε CETT.   4.
ὅθ' αἵ τε ἀπὸ MSS. ὅθεν α.τ.ά. SCHN. E VERS. TURN.   5. θύ-
ραν MSS. ὥραν MAR.VAS. φορὰν FURL. 61 αὖραν TURN.,SCHN. I
7. ταύτην αὐτὴν MSS. τοιαύτην EGO κατ' ὀλίγον MSS. ⟨εὐλο-
γόν ἐστι⟩ SCHN. I E VERS. TURN. κατὰ λόγον SCHN. V.LVII,
WI.   8. δὲ κάδια MSS. ψεκάδια L ALD. λέτριοι HEINS.   9.
γὰρ ὅλως L ALD. γὰρ ἢ ὅλως CETT. γὰρ ὕλη FURL. 61 E VERS.
TURN.

such a wind reaches home to us, we shiver.

24. And for this reason some places, which are depress-
ed and protected against winds from outside, are cold
because of local winds. For the vapor raised by the sun
cannot remain there but moves and creates a breeze. And
so breezes from rivers and lakes and in general those
off the land blow at dawn, when the vapor is becoming
cool from the lack of heat. It is logical that this kind
of breeze should arise because of fair weather among other reasons. When drizzles and light rains fall, the
breezes blow more. For material is added from all sides,
and after that the breezes blow off the land more.

25. Only from the Nile does it appear that no winds blow
or at most slight ones, because the place from which and
the place to which it flows are hot; the breezes arise
when the moisture is condensed. That is why breezes do
not come from a single river in Libya, for they are all
warm. Nor of course do any breezes come from the rivers
around Babylon and Susa or from torrid areas in general.
And yet it is said that the air grows surprisingly cold
towards dawn. This therefore needs to be looked into.
Perhaps the air does grow cold but is not able to advance
and create a breeze, since the areas close at hand which
receive it are hot.

---

25.   3. οὐδὲ τὸν ἐν Λιβύῃ ποταμὸν DEIMOPQRUX₂ οὐδὲ τῶν ἐν
Λ. Z₁ οὐδ' ἀπὸ τῶν ἐν Λιβύῃ ποταμῶν L ALD.,FURL. 61 Λιβίῃ
VAS. οὐδ' DEL. TURN. διὸ καὶ τῶν MAR.VAS.   4. αὖραν DEIMOP
QRUXZ αὔρας L ALD.,CAM. αὖραι SCHN. I οὐδαμῶς MSS. οἴδαμεν
TURN.,MAR.VAS.   9. πορρωτέρως MSS. πορρωτέρω SCHN. I αὖραν
MSS. αὔρας CAM.,FURL. 89 εὐπύρον DIMPQRX₁ εὐπύρων LX₂Z
ALD.,FURL. 61 εὔθυρον U ἐμπύρων TURN.,SCHN. I   10. τούτων
DEIMOPQRX₁ τόπων LUX₂Z ALD.

26.    ἀπὸ γοῦν τῆς ἀπογείας καὶ τῆς τοιαύτης αὔρας καὶ αἱ
τροπαὶ γίνονται, συναθροισθέντος τοῦ ὑγροῦ ἀέρος· ἡ γὰρ
τροπὴ καθάπερ παλιμπνόη τίς ἐστι πνεύματος, ὥσπερ ἐν τοῖς
εὐρίποις τῶν ὑγρῶν· ὅταν γὰρ ἀθροισθῇ καὶ πλῆθος λάβῃ, μεταβάλλει πάλιν εἰς τὸ ἐναντίον. μάλιστα δ' ἐν τοῖς κοίλοις
ταῦτα γίνεται καὶ ὅπου πνέουσιν αἱ ἀπόγειαι. τούτων δ'ἑκάτερον εὐλόγως. ἐν μὲν γὰρ τοῖς κοίλοις ὁ ἀὴρ συναθροιζεται
προσπίπτων,  ἐν δὲ τοῖς ἀναπεπταμένοις διαχεῖται. τῶν δ'
ἀπογείων πνευμάτων ἀσθενὴς ἡ φύσις, ὥστ' οὐ δύνασθαι βιάζεσ-
θαι πόρρω. συμβαίνει δὲ καὶ ἡ ἀνταπόδοσις ἀνάλογον τοῦ τε
πλήθους καὶ τοῦ μεγέθους, ὡς 'ἂν αἱ ἀπόγεαι πνεύσωσιν.
ὁμοίως δὲ καὶ κατὰ τὰς ὥρας, οἷον τὸ ὀψιαίτερον 'ἢ προιαίτερον ἐμβάλλειν αὐτάς.

27.    γίνεται δὲ καὶ ἀνάκλασίς τις τῶν ἀνέμων, ὥστ' ἀντι-
πνεῖν αὐτοῖς ὅταν ὑψηλοτέροις τόποις προσπνεύσαντες ὑπερᾶ-
ραι μὴ δύνωνται, διὸ ἐνιαχοῦ τὰ νέφη τοῖς πνεύμασιν ὑπεναν-
τία φέρεται, καθάπερ περὶ Αἰγείας τῆς Μακεδονίας, βορέου
πνέοντος πρὸς [τὸν] βορέαν. αἴτιον δ' ὅτι τῶν ὀρῶν ὄντων
ὑψηλῶν τῶν τε περὶ τὸν Ὄλυμπον καὶ τὴν Ὄσσαν, τὰ πνεύματα προσπίπτοντα καὶ οὐχ ὑπεραίροντα τούτων ἀνακλᾶται πρὸς
τοὐναντίον. ὥστε καὶ τὰ νέφη κατώτερα ὄντα φέρουσιν ἐναντίως. συμβαίνει δὲ καὶ αὐτὸ τοῦτο παρ' ἄλλοις.

---

26.    1. ἀπογαίας MSS. ἀπογείας SCHN. I    2. [τοῦ ὑγροῦ]
FURL. 89   3. παλιμπνόη Ζ SCHN. I πάλιν περὶ τῶν τρόπων
καλουμένων πνοῇ L ALD. πάλιν πνοῇ FURL. 89   6. ὅπος U καὶ
ὅπως CETT. ὅπου FURL. 62,SCHN. I   7. ἐν μὲν γὰρ τοῖς κοίλοις ὡς συναθροισθήσεται προσπίπτων· ἐν γὰρ τοῖς ἀναπεπταμένοις διαχεῖται MSS. ὁ ἀὴρ ἀθροισθήσεται TURN.,MAR.VAS.
ὅσον ἀθροίζεται προσπίπτον SCHN. IV 694 E VERS. TURN. συν-
αθροίζεται EGO   8. ἐν δὲ SCHN. I   12. τὸ πρότερον DEIMOP
QRUX₁ τὸ προιαίτερον LX₂Z ALD. [τὸ] πρωιαίτερον SCHN. I
13. ἐμβαλλεῖν DXZ ἐμβαλεῖν CETT. ἐμβάλλειν SCHN. I

26. Now reversals originate from land breezes and their like through a concentration of cold air. For the reversing wind is a kind of backflow of the wind, like the waters in situations of ebb and reflux. For when there is a concentration and build-up, there is a change in the opposite direction. This occurs mainly in hollow places and wherever land breezes blow. Each of these has a scientific basis. When the air comes into hollow places, it is concentrated, in open areas it is diffused. Land breezes are weak by nature so that they cannot force their way far. The compensatory motion takes place in proportion to the amount and force of the land winds as they blow. So too with the time of day, that is, whether they blow early or late.

27. There also occurs a backlash of winds so that they blow back against themselves when they flow against high places and cannot rise above them. Therefore the clouds sometimes move in the opposite direction to the winds as in the neighborhood of Aegae in Macedonia, when north wind blows against north wind. The reason is that when the winds blow against the high mountains near Olympus and Ossa and do not surmount them, they lash back in the reverse direction, so that the clouds moving on a lower level move in reverse direction. The same thing happens in other places.

---

27. 1. αὐτοῖς MSS. αὐτοῖς SCHN. I   2. δύνωνται SCHN. I δύνανται CETT.   3. καθάπερ καὶ περὶ MSS. καὶ OM. SCHN. I 4. Λιγγίας MSS. Λυγκέας TURN.,MAR.VAS. Λυγγίας FURL. 89 λυγκεστιδιὰ BON. Αἰγειὰς SCHN. I   5. τὸν MSS. ⌊τὸν⌋ SCHN. I   7. οὐ $X_1Z$ οὔ DEIMOPQRUX$_2$ οὐχ L ALD.,FURL. 62 ὑπεραί- ροντα MAR.VAS.   8. φέρουσιν MSS. φέρονται SCHN. IV 694 φέρεται WOOD-SYMONS

28.  ἐνιαχοῦ δὲ καὶ ὑπ' αὐτοὺς τοὺς ἐτησίας ἀντίπνοαι γίνονται τῷ βορέᾳ διὰ τὴν περίκλασιν, ὥστε καὶ ἐναντιοδρομεῖν τὰ πλοῖα, καθάπερ καὶ περὶ τὸν πόρον τὸν ἐκ Χαλκίδος
εἰς Ὠρωπὸν, οὓς δὴ καλοῦσι παλιμβορέας. γίνεται δὲ τοῦτο
σχεδὸν, ὅταν ὦσι λαμπρότατοι· τότε γὰο μάλιστα δύνανται ὡς
πορρωτάτω διατείνειν, ὅταν πλῆθος ᾖ τὸ ἀντικόπτον. ἐνιαχοῦ
δὲ διὰ τὸ προσκόπτειν σχίζεσθαι συμβαίνει τὸν ἄνεμον, ὥστε τὸ μὲν ἐκεῖσε, τὸ δὲ δεῦρο ῥεῖν, καθάπερ καὶ τὸ ὕδωρ
ὑπὸ μιᾶς πηγῆς καὶ τῆς αὐτῆς ῥέον.

29.  ἁπλῶς δὲ καὶ οἱ τόποι πολλὰς ποιοῦσι τῶν πνευμάτων
μεταβολὰς ἄλλας τε καὶ τὸ σφοδρότερα καὶ ἠρεμέστερα γίνεσ-
θαι· καθάπερ ἐὰν διὰ στενοῦ καὶ ἀχανοῦς πνέῃ. σφοδρότερον
γὰρ ἀεὶ καὶ λαμπρότερον τὸ διὰ τοῦ στενοῦ, καθάπερ ὕδατος
ῥεῖθρον· ἐκβιάζεται γὰρ καὶ διωθεῖ μᾶλλον ἀθρόον. διὸ καὶ
ἐν τοῖς ἄλλοις ἀπνοίας οὔσης, ἐν τοῖς στενοῖς ἀεὶ πνεῦμα.
μένειν γὰρ ὁ ἀὴρ οὐ δύναται διὰ τὸ πλῆθος· ἡ δὲ τούτου κίνησις ἄνεμος. ὅθεν καὶ ἐν τοῖς στενωποῖς, ὅταν κατακλεισ-
θῶσι καὶ συμπέσωσι, λαμπροὶ πνέουσι· καὶ ἐν ταῖς πύλαις.
καὶ αἱ θυρίδες ἕλκουσιν ἀεὶ, καὶ πνοὴν παρέχουσι· πάντων
γὰρ τούτων καὶ τῶν τοιούτων ἡ αὐτὴ καὶ μία τις ἡ εἰρημένη
αἰτία.

30.  πάλιν δ' ἔνιοι τόποι διὰ τὴν κοιλότητα καὶ διὰ τὸ
περιέχεσθαι μείζοσιν, ἐγγὺς ὄντες γε 'ἢ ἐγγυτέρω ἑτέρων

28.  2. ἀντιδρομεῖν L ALD. ἀντιδραμεῖν MAR.VAS.,FURL. 89
ἐναντιοδρομεῖν CETT.,SCHN. I  3. πόρθμον FURL. 62  4.
ἰσορροπον DEIMOPQUX₁Z  εἰς ὁρωπὸν LX₂ ALD. εἰς Ὠρωπὸν
SCHN. I παλιμβορέας Z SCHN. I πάλιν βορέας CETT.  5. λαμ-
πρότατα MSS. λαυρότατα FURL. 90 λαμπρότατοι SCHN. I δύνανται EMO SCHN. I δύναται CETT.  6. ἀντικόπον MSS. ἀντικόπτον FURL. 62,SCHN. I  7. σχίζειν MSS. σχίζεσθαι SCHN. I

29.  2. ἄλλως τε καὶ MSS. ἄλλα τε καὶ TURN. ἄλλας τε καὶ
SCHN. I  6. ἀπνοίας LXZ FURL. 62 ἀπονοίας CETT.  9. συμ-
πεσοῦσι MSS. συμπέσωσι SCHN. I

28. Sometimes too at about the time of the etesians,
winds arise counter to the north wind because of a cir-
cling back so that ships move in the opposite direction,
as is true of the passage from Chalcis to Oropus. These
winds are called reverse north winds. This happens especially when the winds blow most vigorously. For at that
time they are most able to reach farthest, when the reversing wind is massive. Sometimes the wind happens to
divide because it hits an obstacle, flowing this side
and that, like water welling up from the same single
source.

29. In sum, topography accounts for many changes in
winds, including the degree of force or gentleness. Example: whether they blow through a narrow and constrict-
ed place. For a wind passing through a gap is always
more forceful and vigorous like a current of water.
Concentrated, it has more thrust. That is why, when
there is a calm elsewhere, wind is always present in
narrow passages. The wind cannot stand still because of
its mass. But the movement of air is wind. Hence, if
winds are confined and concentrated in narrow passages,
they blow hard, likewise in portals. Windows also pull
in air and create a breeze. The cause of all these phenomena and their like is one and the same, the one already stated.

30. Again, some places which are near or at least nearer
than other places to the sources are altogether windless

---

30.    1. πολὺν Z πόλιν DMPQUX πάλιν CETT. 2. ὄντος MSS.
ὄντες BON.,FURL. 63 ὄντες ἐγγυτέρω FURL. 90 ἕτερον MSS.
OM. BON. ἑτέρων SCHN. I 3. ἀπόπνως MSS. ἄπνοοι TURN. VEL
ἀπνοὶ MAR.VAS. ἀποπνεύματοι SCHN.    7. οὐδ᾽ ἐπίπροσθεν
MSS. οὐδὲν ἐπίπροσθεν MAR.VAS. οὐδ᾽ ἐπιπροσθεῖται ἡ φορὰ
BON. ἐπίπροσθεν LAC. 13-23 LITT ἡ φορὰ MSS. FORT. καὶ οὐ

ταῖς ἀρχαῖς. ὅλως ἄπνοοι τυγχάνουσιν·οἱ δὲ πορρωτέρω πνευ-
ματώδεις, ὥσπερ καὶ περὶ Θετταλίαν καὶ Μακεδονίαν κατὰ
τοὺς ἐτησίας. οὐ γὰρ πνέουσι παρ' αὐτοῖς, ὡς εἰπεῖν·ἐν δὲ
ταῖς νήσοις λαμπροὶ ταῖς μακρὰν ἀπηρτημέναις. αἴτιον δὲ τὸ
τὰς χώρας κοίλας καὶ ἐπισκεπεῖς εἶναι· ταῖς δὲ νήσοις οὐδὲν ἐπίπροσθεν τῆς φορᾶς. κωλύονται δὲ καὶ οὗτοι καὶ ὅλως
πᾶς ἄνεμος πνεῖν 'ἢ διὰ τὴν ἀπόστασιν, (οὐ γὰρ δύνανται
διατείνειν εἰς τὸ πορρωτέρω διὰ τὸ μῆκος) 'ἢ δι' ἐπιπρόσ-
θησίν τινων, 'ἢ τρίτον εἴ τι πνεῦμα ἐγχώριον ἀντιπνεῖ καὶ
κρατεῖ.

31.   ὅτι δὲ συμβαίνει κατὰ τὴν ὥραν τοὺς ἐτησίας ἐπαίρεσθαι καὶ τὴν τροπαίαν πνεῖν περὶ Μακεδονίαν, ὥσπερ σύμπτωμα
θετέον· πανταχοῦ γὰρ τῆς μεσημβρίας ἀπολήγει τὰ πνεύματα
διὰ τὸν ἥλιον, ἅμα δὲ τῇ δείλῃ πάλιν αἴρεται. συμβαίνει δὲ
κατὰ τὸν αὐτὸν καιρὸν τήν τε τροπαίαν πρὸς ταῖς ἀπογείαις
αὔραις καὶ τοὺς ἐτησίας ἐπαίρεσθαι πάλιν.   οὐ γὰρ δὴ τὴν
ἀνάκλασιν τὴν ἀπὸ τοῦ Ὀλύμπου καὶ τῆς Ὄσσης τῶν ἐτησίων
αἰτιατέον, 'ἢν μὴ ἠρεμαῖοι ὦσιν 'ἢ μέτριοι παντελῶς. τὰ
μὲν οὖν συμπτώματα πειρατέον ἅπασι διαιρεῖν.

32.   ἐκεῖνο δ' 'ἂν δόξειεν ἄτοπον καὶ παράλογον εἶναι, διὰ
τί τῶν ὑψηλῶν τόπων τὰ μὲν προσήνεμα πάντα ἀπνεύματα τυγχάνει,   τὰ δ' ἐπισκεπῆ πνευματώδη καὶ οὐ μετρίως,   ἀλλὰ
σφοδρῶς, οἷον ἐν Πλαταιαῖς τῆς Βοιωτίας, κειμέναις πρὸς

κωλύεται ἡ φορὰ FURL. 90 τῆς φορᾶς SCHN. I E VERS. TURN.
10. εἰ δι' LX₂Z ALD. εἰ δ' X₁CETT. ἐπίπροσθεσιν MSS. ἐπι-
πρόσθησιν MAR.VAS. 'ἢ τὸ EIMOPQRUX₁ εἰ τὸ DLX₂Z εἴ τι
MAR.VAS.

31.   1. ὅτε MSS. ὅτι SCHN. I   5. πρὸν XZ πρὶν DEIMOPQRU
πρὸς L ALD.,FURL. 63   6. τοῖς ἐτησίαις BON. οὐ γὰρ δὴ
DEIMOPQRXZ οὐ γὰρ διὰ U οὐδὲ γὰρ L ALD.,CAM. δὴ OM. SCHN.
I, REST. SCHN. V 160   7. τῆς ἀπὸ MSS. τὴν ἀπὸ MAR.VAS.
8. 'ἢν MSS. 'ἢν SCHN. I ἑρμηνεύουσι MSS.,MAR.VAS. ἐρίνε-
μοί εἰσιν FURL. 63 'ἢν μὴ ἠρεμαῖοι ὦσιν 'ἢ μέτριοι παν-

because they are in hollows and are surrounded by higher
ground. Places farther off have wind, as happens in
Thessaly and Macedonia at the time of the etesians. These
do not blow in their own territory, as it were, but in
the islands which are far removed they are vigorous. The
reason is that the homeland is sunken and protected,
while in the islands there is no obstacle to the movement. These winds, and, generally speaking, every wind,
are prevented from blowing either by remoteness (for they
cannot reach far because of the distance), or by inter-
position of obstacles, or thirdly by some local wind
blowing counter and dominating.

31. The fact that the etesians rise and the reversing
winds blow at the same time should be considered as being
in conjunction. For everywhere at noon the winds die
down because of the sun's action, and arise again with
the late afternoon. It happens that the reversing wind
blows against the land winds and the etesians rise at
the same time again. For we must not lay the cause of
the etesians to bouncing back from Olympus and Ossa if
they are not becalmed or are quite moderate. We must try
to determine the conjunctions for all cases individually.

32. There is the strange and puzzling question why those
high places which face the wind are calm while those
which are protected are windy and forcefully so. For
example, in Plataea in Boeotia, which faces the north

---

τελῶς CORAY APUD SCHN. V 160 'ἢ μέτριοι SCHN. V,LVII παντελῶς OM. SCHN. I, REST. V 160

32. 1. δόξαιεν FURL. 91  3. ἐπισκοπῇ MSS. ἐπισκεπῇ BON.
FURL. 63 μετρίου FURL. 63  4. κειμένης MSS. κειμένοις
VAS. κειμέναις FURL. 63  7. τῆς ἐτησίας MSS. τοὺς ἐτη-

τὸν βορέαν, ὁ μὲν βορέας εὐδιεινός, ὁ δὲ νότος μέγας καὶ
χειμερινός, καὶ ἐπιπροσθοῦντος τοῦ Κιθαιρῶνος. καὶ πάλιν
παρὰ μὲν τὰ κοῖλα τῆς Εὐβοίας ὑπὸ τοὺς ἐτησίας τροπαῖαι
παραθέουσιν, ἐν Καρύστῳ δὲ τηλικοῦτοι πνέουσιν, ὥστε ἐξαί-
σιον εἶναι μέγεθος.

33. ἔτι δὲ τῆς Κουριάδος ἐν τῷ καλουμένῳ Φαι⟨στῷ τῷ⟩
κειμένῳ πρὸς νότον, ὑψηλῷ καὶ ἀποτομῷ, θαυμαστόν τι κῦμα
μὲν εἰσπίπτει, πνεῦμα δ' οὐκ ἔστιν. ἀλλὰ καὶ τὰ πλοῖα
προσορμίζονται τοῖς λειοτάτοις ⟨τόποις⟩ ἀλιμένων ⟨ὄντων
τῶν⟩ πλησίον, καὶ τὰ συμβαίνοντα θεωρεῖν ἐστι. αἴτιον δὲ
τοῦ μὲν μὴ διικνεῖσθαι τὸ πνεῦμα πρὸς τὴν γῆν, τὸ μὴ ὑπ-
άγειν τὸν ἀέρα, μηδὲ ῥεῖν· ὅπερ συμβαίνει διὰ τὸ ὕψος·
προσκό⟨πτει γὰρ⟩ οὐχ ὑπεραίρων. ὅτι δ' ὑπεξάγειν ἀεὶ δεῖ,
καὶ μὴ ἵστασθαι τὸν ἀέρα, φανερόν. ἐν γὰρ τοῖς οἰκήμασιν,
εἴ τις 'ἂν κατακλείσῃ τὰς θύρας, ἧττον διὰ θυρίδων ἡ πνοὴ
φέρεται. πλῆρες γὰρ 'ὂν, καὶ μὴ ὑπεξάγον, οὐκ εἰσδέχεται
τὸν ἔξωθεν ἀέρα· πρὸς γὰρ τὸ κενὸν ἡ φορά. διὸ καὶ τὸ ἕλ-
κειν οὐ καλῶς λέγεται.

σίας MAR.VAS.,SCHN. I τρόπαιαν MSS. τροπαῖαι MAR.VAS.,
SCHN. I   8. οὐ παραθέουσιν TURN. καρίστῳ MSS. Καρύστῳ
SCHN. I   9. τὸ μέγεθος FURL. 91

33.   1. ο ἔτι D φαι LAC. 13 LITT. MSS. FELLUM FURL. 92
Φαιστῷ SCHN. V,LVII,WI.   3. πνεῦμα δ' οὐδέποτε, ἀλλὰ καὶ
τὰ πλοῖα SCHN. V 161   4. προσορμίζοντα MSS. προσορμίζον-
ται SCHN. I ⟨τόποις⟩ EGO ἀλιμένων L ALD.,SCHN. I ἀλειμένων
CETT. ὄντων τῶν τόπων καὶ οὐδέποτ' οὐδὲ τὰ πλοῖα προσορμίζοντα τοῖς λειωτοῖς ἀλειμένων πλήσια P ⟨ἀλλὰ⟩ FURL. 64
τοῖς λιμέσιν ἀλιμένοις FURL. 92 SED ET NAVIGIA BONA LENI-
QUE TEMPESTATE AD LOCA PROPE IMPORTUOSA APPELLUNTUR IDQUE
VIDERE LICET TURN. QUIN ET NAVES UT PORTUM APPELLUNT,
QUASI IN PORTU NON SINT, AGITARI VIDEAS, ATQUE HUIUS GEN-
ERIS EVENTA FURL. 64 καὶ τοῖς κλειστοῖς τῶν λιμένων παρα-
πλήσια τὰ συμβαίνοντα θεωρεῖν SCHN. IV 697 ἀλιμένων ὄντων
τῶν τόπων τῶν πλησίον καὶ τὰ συμβαίνοντα θεωρεῖν ἐστι

wind, the wind is mild, while the south wind is strong
and stormy, even though Mt. Cithaeron blocks it off.
Again, at the time of the etesians the reverse winds by-
pass the hollow districts, whereas at Carystus they blow
so hard that their strength is extraordinary.

33. Also, in the place called Phaestus in the Curiad
district, to the south, which is elevated and scarped, an
immense wave breaks, though there is no wind. However,
ships make anchorage at the least rocky places, since the
neighborhood has no harbors, and are able to watch the
event. The reason the wind does not reach the land is
that the air does not withdraw or flow (away). This is
because of the elevation. The wind encounters this air
but does not rise above it. We can see that the air must
always recede and not stand still. Notice that when the
doors in a house are closed, the breeze through the windows is cut down. The house being full of air which does
not give place, air from outside cannot get in. For the
motion runs toward the void. For that reason, "drawing
air" is not an appropriate expression.

---

SCHN. V 161   6. τὸ μὴ EO SCHN. I τῷ μὴ CETT.   7. μὴ δέ-
ρειν MSS. μηδὲ ῥεῖν MAR.VAS. αἴρειν FURL. 64 πρὸς κα LAC.
19 LITT. MSS. πρὸς κάτω FURL. 92 οὐχι περαίρω MSS. οὐχι
περαιτέρω M οὐχ ὑπεραίρων L ALD.,FURL. 64 πρόσω οὐχ ὑπερ-
αἴρων TURN.,MAR.VAS. OBSTANTEM ALTITUDINEM NON SUPERANS
TURN. ὕψος πρὸς κ΄ στάδια οὐχ ὑ. STEIN. 47 ἔτι DEIMOPQR
X₁ ὅτι LX₂Z ALD. προσκόπτων γὰρ οὐχ ὑπεραιρει SCHN. IV
προσκόπτει γὰρ EGO   10. οὔτις 'ἀν MSS. εἴ τις 'ἀν BON.
11.ὑπεξάγοντος ⟨τοῦ ἀέρος⟩ SCHN. IV 697

34.   τὰ δὲ πρὸς βορέαν καὶ ὅλως κατ' ἀνέμους ἐπισκεπῆ διὰ
τοῦτο πνευματωδέστερα, διότι συμβαίνει συναθροιζόμενον ἐπὶ
τὸ ὕψος οἷον ὑπερχεῖσθαι τὸ πνεῦμα, καὶ ἐμπίπτειν ἀθρόον.
ἢ γὰρ 'ἂν ἐπιβρίσῃ, ταύτῃ κατέρρηξεν ⌊ἀληθῶς⌋ ἀθρόον. γίνονται δὲ καὶ αἱ καταιγίδες ἐν τοῖς τοιούτοις. συστροφὴ γὰρ
ἐνταῦθα καὶ ἀθροισμὸς πνεύματος. ὥσθ' ὅταν ἐκραγῇ, καθάπερ
πληγὴν ἐποίησεν. ἰσχυρὸν γὰρ τὸ ἀθρόον καὶ συνεχές, ὥσπερ
καὶ ἐπὶ τῶν τυφώνων. 'ἃ μὲν οὖν διὰ τοὺς ·τόπους συμβαίνει,
ταῦτα καὶ τοιαῦτα τυγχάνει. πολλὰ δ' ἐστι καὶ πολλαχοῦ,
περὶ ὧν ἑκάστου τῆς ἱστορίας λέγειν

35.   τὰ δὲ τοιάδε κοινὰ πάντων τῶν ἀνέμων οἷον ὅσα σημει-
ώδη καθ' ἕκαστον ἐν τῷ μέλλειν.ὁ γὰρ ἀὴρ ἀλλοιούμενος κατὰ πυκνότητα καὶ μανότητα,'ἢ κατὰ θερμότητα καὶ ψύξιν,'ἢ
κατ' ἄλλην τινὰ τοιαύτην διάθεσιν, ἐξεδήλωσεν ἀεὶ τὴν ἐπι-
οῦσαν πνοήν· ὁμοιοπαθῆ γὰρ τὰ κατὰ τὸν ἀέρα, καὶ προτερεῖ
τῶν ἀνέμων εἰς τὴν ἡμετέραν αἴσθησιν. ὡσαύτως δὲ καὶ ἐπὶ
τῆς θαλάττης καὶ τῶν ὑδάτων ἐστί τισι τὰ αὐτὰ σημεῖα λα-
βεῖν· ἐπεὶ καὶ τὰ κύματα προανιστάμενα καὶ προεκπίπτοντα
σημαίνει τοὺς ἀνέμους. προωθεῖται δὲ ⟨οὐ⟩ συνεχῶς ἀλλὰ κατὰ μικρόν. τοῦτο δὲ προωθεῖ ἄλλο, 'ὃ προέωσε· καὶ πάλιν
⟨'ὃ προέωσε δι'⟩ ἄλλης πνοῆς ἐκινήθη, μαρανθείσης τῆς πρω-
της· εἶθ' οὕτως ἀεὶ προωθούμενα προσέρχεται. παρόντος δὲ

34.   1. βοράν MSS. βορράν MAR.VAS. βορέαν SCHN. I κατήν-
υμα MSS. κατ' ἄνεμον MAR.VAS. κατηνέμων BON. κατήνεμα
SCHN. I κατ' ἀνέμους WI. ⟨καὶ⟩ SCHN. I QUAE AUTEM ADVERSUS
BOREAM ATQUE ADEO VENTOS ALIOS TECTA SUNT   TURN.  2.πνευ-
ματωδέστερα M SCHN. I πνευματοδέστερα CETT. διὸ MSS. διότι
TURN.,MAR.VAS.    4. LAC. 28 LITT. ἢ γὰρ DEIMOQUZ κῶς ἢ γὰρ
LP ALD. ἐπικυρίσῃ DILMQRUXZ ἐπικηρίσῃ O ἐπιβρίσῃ P TURN.,
MAR.VAS. ἐπικύφῃ FURL. 93 κατέραξεν MSS. κατήρραξεν SCHN.
I κατέρρηξεν SCHN. V,LVII,WI. ⌊ἀληθῶς ἀθρόον⌋ SCHN. V 161
[ἀληθῶς] EGO    5. συστροφὴ MSS. συστροφαὶ SCHN. I γὰρ OM.
CAM.    6. ἐνραγῇ L ALD.,CAM.    9. FORT. καὶ ⟨τοιαῦτα⟩
SCHN. IV 698   10. λέγειν L ALD. λέγει CETT.

34. Localities protected against the north wind (and
winds in general) are for that reason windier because it
happens that the wind is gathered aloft and in a sense
overflows and descends in a body. Wherever the wind
presses downward, it rushes below in concentration. In
such cases squalls ensue. Here sudden storms and concentrations of wind occur, so that when the wind breaks
forth, it has the effect of a shock. For concentrated
wind is powerful and continuous, as with whirlwinds.
Thus these and like phenomena take place because of local
features. There are many such occurrences in many places,
whose details are the subject of investigation.

35. The following features are common to all winds, such
as what signs indicate the coming of each wind. For air,
by altering with respect to density and rarity, heat or
cold, or any other condition, always reveals the coming
breeze. For the winds are in key with the air, and the
air precedes the wind in affecting our senses. Similarly, it is possible for some people to take in these same
signs on the ocean and on fresh-water bodies. The waves,
by rising and falling in advance, signify the coming
winds. The waves are pushed forward at intervals, not
uninterruptedly; one wave pushes the other, which pushes
a third; in turn, as the first wave dies, the next wave

---

35. 2. ἕκαστον, SUBAUDIENDUM τόπον SCHN. IV 698 ἀχλυού-
μενος MSS. ἀλλοιούμενος BON. ἀχλυόμενον FURL. 64    3. μὴ
κατ’ ἄλλην MSS. ’ἢ κατ’ BON. 5. προτυρεῖ P προτηρεῖ CETT.
προτερεῖ MAR.VAS. 6. τὸν ἄνεμον MSS. τῶν ἀνέμων MAR.VAS.
SCHN. I 9. προωθεῖ ταῖς LAC. 12 LITT. EIMOPQRU ALD LAC.
18 LITT. DLXZ ⟨οὐ⟩ MAR.VAS.    10. ἀλλ’ ὁ MSS. ἄλλο ‘ὁ MAR.
VAS. προῶσε DILMPQRUXZ προῶσαι CETT. προέωσε SCHN. I τὸ
μὲν οὖν πρῶτον προωθεῖ καὶ πάλιν τοῦτο, ‘ὁ πρέωσε δι’ ἀλ-
λης πνοῆς SCHN. IV 699 ⟨προέωσε δι’⟩ SCHN. LAC. MSS. 11.

τοῦ κινουμένου φανερὸν ὅτι καὶ τὸ κινοῦν ἥξει. συμβαίνει
δὴ καὶ ὑστερεῖν τὰ κύματα τῶν πνευμάτων· ὕστερον γὰρ δια-
λύονται καὶ παρακμάζουσι, διὰ τὸ δυσκινητότερον καὶ δυσ-
καταπαυστότερον.

36. κοινὰ δὲ καὶ τὰ τοιαῦτα πλειόνων, οἷον ἀστέρων τε
καὶ ⟨σελήνης⟩ καὶ ἄλων καὶ παρηλίων φάσις καὶ ἀπομάρανσις
ἢ ῥῆξις, καὶ εἴ τι τοιοῦθ᾿ ἕτερον. πρότερον γὰρ ὁ ἀὴρ ὁ
ἄνω τῷ πάσχειν ἀποδηλοῖ τὴν τῶν πνευμάτων φύσιν. ἔτι δὲ τὸ
ἐπὶ τέλει μεγίστους εἶναι· καὶ γὰρ τοῦτο κοινὸν πλείοσιν.
ὅταν γὰρ ἀθρόον ἐκπνεύσωσιν, μικρὸν γίνεται τὸ λοιπον. τὰ
μὲν οὖν τοιαῦτα, καθάπερ εἴρηται, κοινά πως τῆς οὐσίας.

37. ἔστι δὲ τὰ καθ᾿ ἕκαστον ἴδια κατὰ τὴν ἑκάστου φύσιν
καὶ θέσιν, ὧν τὰ μὲν τοῖς τόποις μερίζεται, καθ᾿ οὓς καὶ
πρὸς οὓς αἱ πνοαί, τὰ δὲ ταῖς ἀρχαῖς, ἀφ᾿ ὧν, τὰ δὲ ἄλλοις
τοιούτοις. ἰδιώτατα δ᾿ οὖν, ὡς εἰπεῖν, τὰ περὶ τὸν καικίαν
καὶ τὰ περὶ τὸν ζέφυρόν ἐστιν. ὁ μὲν γὰρ καικίας μόνος ἐφ᾿
αὐτὸν ἄγει τὰ νέφη καθάπερ καὶ παροιμία λέγει, ἕλκων ἐφ᾿

ὑπ᾿ ἄλλης MAR.VAS.,BON. προωθουμένης MSS. προωθούμενα
FURL. 64    13. συμβαίνει δὴ καὶ τὰ κύματα ὑστερεῖν $Z_1$ σ.δ.
κ. ὑστερεῖν τὰ κύματα CETT. δὲ καὶ FURL. 94,SCHN. II 592,
WI.  14. ὕστερον MSS. ὕστερον γὰρ SCHN. II 592   15. διὰ
τὸ $LX_2Z$ ALD. τοίαι CETT. δυσκινητότερον WOOD-SYMONS δυσ-
καταπαυστότατον Z δυσκατακαυστότερον CETT.

36.  1. τελις LAC. 16 LITT. σκε ἄλλων καὶ παρ᾿ ἡλίῳ MSS.
ἀστέρας διάττοντες καὶ ἄλωνας TURN. οἷον ἀστέρων καὶ ἄλλων φάσις VEL ἀστέρων τε ὁλκὸς ἄλων καὶ παρηλίων MAR.VAS.
τε καὶ σελήνης καὶ ἄλλων FURL. 64 τε καὶ OM. FURL. 94   2.
παρ᾿ ἡλίῳ MSS. παρηλίων SCHN. Ι ἀστέρων τε διαττόντων καὶ
παρηλίων WI.  3. ἐπὶ τοιοῦθ᾿ ἕστερον DEIMOPQRUXZ ἕτερον
L ALD.,FURL. 64 καὶ εἴ τι τοιοῦθ᾿ TURN. καὶ εἴ τι τοιοῦτο
ἕτερον MAR.VAS. ὁ ἀὴρ ἄνω τὸ MSS. ὁ ἀὴρ ὁ ἄνω τῷ BON.   4.
ἔστι MSS. ἔτι FURL. 65   5. μεγίστους MSS. μέγιστος FURL.
65 ἔστι δὲ καὶ ἐπὶ τέλει μεγίστους FURL. 95 ἔστι MSS.
εἶναι SCHN. Ι τούτοις κενὸν MSS. τοῦτο κοινὸν TURN.,

is pushed by another breeze. Thus then they come on as
they are pushed forward. When that which is being moved
appears, it is clear that the moving force will arrive.
And it also happens that waves persist after the winds,
for they crest and break up later, since they are more
difficult to set in motion or to bring to a halt once
they are in motion.

36. The following are also common to many winds, such
as the appearance and the fading or breakup of stars,
moon, haloes, mock-suns, and any other such phenomenon.
For what happens to the upper air foretells what the
wind will be like. There is also the fact that winds
are very strong at the end. This is common to many
winds. For when they blow themselves out in concentrated
mass, there is little left. Such phenomena then are in
some way common to the nature of the winds, as has been
said.

37. The peculiarities of each wind depend  on its nature
and position. Some are due to the places over which and
towards which the breezes blow, some to the source of the
breeze, some to other such factors. Most special, we may
say, are the characteristics of the east-north-east wind
and those of the west wind. The east-north-east wind
draws clouds to itself; as the proverb puts it: "drawing
clouds to himself like the east-north-east wind."

---

MAR.VAS.    6. ἐμπνεύσωσιν MSS. ἐκπνεύσωσιν BON. E PROB.
26,25

37.   3. αἱ πνοαὶ MSS. 'ἂν πνοαὶ BAS., FORT. 'ἂν αἱ πνοαὶ
SCHN. IV 700 ὑφ' ὧν MSS. ἀφ' ὧν MAR.VAS.,SCHN. I   4. ἀπ-
αρκτίαν MSS. καικίαν MAR.VAS.,BON. κα·ι·κίαν SALMASIUS
1259 5. ἀπαρκτίας MSS. καικίας MAR.VAS.,BON. ἑαυτὸν DEIMO
PQRUXZ αὐτὸν L ALD. αὐτὸν CAM.,SCHN.  7. νέφη L ALD.,SCHN.
I νέφος CETT.,PROB. 26,29

αὐτὸν ὥστε καικίας νέφη.

38. ὁ δὲ ζέφυρος λειότατος τῶν ἀνέμων, καὶ πνεῖ δείλης
καὶ ἐπὶ τὴν γῆν, καὶ ψυχρός, τῶν ἐνιαυσίων ἐν δυοῖν μόνον
ὥραις, ἐαρινῇ καὶ μετοπώρου. πνεῖ δ' ἐνιαχοῦ μὲν χειμέριος
(ὅθεν καὶ ὁ ποιητὴς δυσαῆ προσηγόρευσεν)· ἐνιαχοῦ δὲ μέτριος καὶ μαλακός. διὸ καὶ Φιλόξενος ἡδεῖαν αὐτοῦ πεποίηκε
τὴν πνοήν. ⟨ καὶ τοὺς καρποὺς⟩ τοὺς μὲν ἐκτρέφει, τοὺς δ'
ἀπολλύει καὶ διαφθείρει τελείως.

39. αἴτιον δὲ τῷ μὲν καικίᾳ, διότι πέφυκε κυκλοτερεῖ φέ-
ρεσθαι γραμμῇ, ἧς τὸ κοῖλον πρὸς τὸν οὐρανὸν καὶ οὐκ ἐπὶ
τὴν γῆν ἐστιν, ὥσπερ τῶν ἄλλων, διὰ τὸ κάτωθεν πνεῖν·πνέ-
ων δ' ἐπὶ τὴν ἀρχὴν οὕτως ἐφ' αὐτὸν ἄγει τὰ νέφη.πρὸς 'ὃ
γὰρ ἡ πνοὴ, καὶ τῶν νεφῶν ἐντεῦθεν ⟨ἡ⟩ φορά.

40. ὁ δὲ ζέφυρος ψυχρὸς μὲν διὰ τὸ πνεῖν ἀφ'ἑσπέρας ἀπὸ
θαλάττης καὶ πεδίων ἀναπεπταμένων, καὶ ἔτι μετὰ ⟨τὸν⟩ χειμῶνα τοῦ ἦρος, ἄρτι τοῦ ἡλίου κρατοῦντος, καὶ μετοπώρου
πάλιν, ὅτ' οὐκέτι κρατεῖ ⟨ὁ ἥλιος⟩. τοῦ δὲ βορέου ἧττον
ψυχρὸς διὰ τὸ ἀφ' ὕδατος πνευματουμένου καὶ μὴ χιόνος
πνεῖν. οὐ συνεχὴς δὲ, διὰ τὸ μὴ κρατεῖσθαι τὸ γινόμενον
πνεῦμα. οὐ γὰρ ὥσπερ ἐν ⟨τῇ⟩ γῇ ⟨ὑπομένει τὴν εἴλην⟩,ἀλλὰ
πλανᾶται, διὰ τὸ ἐφ' ὑγροῦ βεβηκέναι.

---

38. 1. δεινῶς L ALD. δειλῶς CETT. δείλης BON.,SCHN. I E
PROB. 26,35   3. ἐαρινὴν U ἐαρινῇ LXZ ALD. ἔαρος M ἐάρειν
CETT. ἐαρινῇ FURL. 65,SCHN. I μέτριος Z$_2$ SCHN. I μετρίως
Z$_1$CETT.   5. ⟨ἐστι⟩ WI. μαλακὸς X$_2$ SCHN. I μαλακῶς X$_1$CETT.
ἰδίαν MSS. ἡδεῖαν WI.   6. ⟨καὶ τῶν καρπῶν⟩ FURL. 65,SCHN.
I ⟨καὶ τοὺς καρποὺς⟩ E 43,3 EGO τοῖς μὲν MSS. τοὺς μὲν
FURL. 65 τοῖς δὲ MSS. τοὺς δὲ FURL. 65   7. ἀποκλείει
MSS. ἀπολλύει FURL. 65 διαφέρει MSS. διαφθείρει MAR.VAS.,
FURL. 65

39. 2. ἧς τὸ LX$_2$Z ALD. εἰς τὸ CETT. οὐ περὶ MSS. οὐκ ἐπὶ
BON.   4. ἀρχὴν LAC. 18 LITT. MSS. οὗτος ἐφ' ἑαυτὸν MSS.
οὕτως MAR.VAS.   5. ⟨ἡ⟩ SCHN. I

38. The west wind is the mildest of the winds; it blows
in two seasons only, the spring and the late autumn. In
some places it is stormy, which is why the poet called
it "ill-blowing"; in some places it is moderate and gentle, for which reason Philoxenus said that its breeze is
sweet. Some crops it nourishes, some it destroys completely.

39. The reason for the behavior of the east-north-east
wind is that it moves in a circle, whose concavity faces
skyward and not earthward like the others, since it blows
away from the earth. Blowing thus towards its starting
point it draws the clouds towards itself. For the movement of the clouds is from the place toward which the
wind blows.

40. The west wind is cold because it blows from the
west and from the sea and the open plains, also coming
hard upon winter in the spring, while the sun is beginning to control; and again in the late autumn, when the
sun no longer controls. It is less cold than the north
wind, because it blows off vaporizing water, not snow.
It is not continuous, because the wind is not controlled
as it generates. For it does not await the warmth as on
land but moves around because it has passed over water.

------

40. 2. ⟨τὸν⟩ FURL. 65,SCHN. I   4. πάλιν OM. FURL. 96
κρατεῖς FURL. 65 ⟨ὁ ἥλιος⟩ FURL. 65,SCHN. I ⟨δὲ⟩ MAR.VAS.,
FURL. 65 τοῦ Βορέου δ᾽HEINS. QUOD GENERATUS SPIRITUS MI-
NIME COHIBETUR TURN. 7. ⟨τῇ⟩ SCHN. I ⟨ὑπομένει τὴν ὕλ-
ην⟩ BON. ⟨ὑπομένει τὴν εἴλην⟩ EGO E PROB. 26,25   8. διὰ
τὸ ἐφ᾽ ὑγροῦ βεβηκέναι MSS. διὰ τὸ ἀφ᾽ ὑγροῦ ⟨πνευματου-
μένου⟩ μεταβεβηκέναι SCHN. II 593

41.    καὶ ὁμαλὸς διὰ τοῦτό ἐστιν. οὐ γὰρ ⟨ἀπ' ὀρέων πνεῖ
οὐδὲ βίᾳ τηκομένου, ἀλλὰ ῥᾳδίως⟩ [βορέαν καὶ νότον πρὸς
ἑσπέραν δ' οὐκ οὐδέ τις ἐστί] ὥσπερ δι' αὐλοῦ ῥέων. τὰ
μὲν γὰρ πρὸς βορέαν καὶ νότον ⟨ὀρεινά, τὰ⟩ πρὸς ἑσπέραν
δ' οὔτε ὄρος οὔτε γῆ ἐστιν, ἀλλὰ τὸ Ἀτλαντικὸν πέλαγος,
ὥστε ἐπὶ τῆς γῆς φέρεται. τῆς δείλης ⟨δὲ⟩ ἡ πνοὴ διὰ τὸν
τόπον. πάντα γὰρ μετὰ τοῦ ἡλίου, διαχέοντος τὸ ὑγρὸν 'ἡ
ἀτμίζοντος γίνεται καὶ συνεργοῦντος εἰς τὴν ἀρχήν. ὅταν
οὖν εἰς τὸν τόπον ἀφίκηται, καὶ ἡ πνοὴ ⟨ἄρχεται⟩. καὶ τῆς
νυκτὸς παύεται, διὰ τὸ ἐλλείπειν τὴν τοῦ ἡλίου κίνησιν.

42.    ἄγει δὲ καὶ νεφέλας μεγίστας, ὅτι ἐκ πελάγους πνεῖ
καὶ κατὰ θάλατταν, ὥστε ἐκ πολλοῦ συνάγειν. χειμέριος δὲ
καὶ δυσαὴς, διά τε τὰ πρότερον εἰρημένα. μετὰ γὰρ τὸν χειμῶνα πνεῖ ψυχροῦ ἔτι τοῦ ἀέρος ὄντος. ἐπεὶ ὁ μετοπωρινὸς
οὐ τοιοῦτος, εἰ μὴ τῷ μεγέθει λαμβάνοι τις τὸ χειμέριον.

41.    1-10. καὶ ἐφ' ὁμαλῆς διὰ τοῦτο ἐστιν. οὐ γὰρ LAC. 5-
14 LITT. βορίαν (βορέαν DLXZ ALD.) καὶ νότον πρὸς ἑσπέραν
οὐκ (οὐχ DXZ) οὐδέ τις ἐστί LAC. 5-7 LITT. περ (ὥσπερ MZ)
δι' αὐλοῦ ῥέων. τὴν (δι' αὐτὴν L ALD.) μὲν γὰρ πρὸς βορέαν
καὶ νότον πρὸς ἑσπέραν οὐκ (οὐχ DXZ) ἕτερος οὐδέ τις ἐστί.
ἀλλὰ τὸ Ἀτλαντικὸν πέλαγος ὥστε ἐπὶ τῆς γῆς φέρεται. τῆς
δείλης ἡ πνοὴ διὰ τὸν τόπον· πάντα γὰρ μετὰ τοῦ ἡλίου διαχέοντος τὸ ὑγρὸν 'ἡ ἀτμίζοντος γίνεται 'ἡ συνεργοῦντος εἰς
τὴν ἀρχήν· ὅταν (ὅτε DL) οὖν εἰς τὸν τόπον ἀφίκηται· καὶ
πνοὴ καὶ (OM. EOR) τῆς νυκτὸς παύεται διὰ τὸ ἐλλείπειν τὴν
τοῦ ἡλίου κίνησιν MSS.    1. καὶ ὁμαλὸς BON. τὸ ἀφ' ὑγροῦ
μεταβεβηκέναι ἀφ' ὁμαλῇ· διὰ τοῦτο καὶ λεῖός ἐστιν·οὐ γὰρ
ἀπ'ὀρέων πνεῖ SCHN.V,LVII (οὐ γὰρ δι'((ἀπ'WI.)) ὀρέων πνεῖ
οὐδὲ βίᾳ τηκομένου, ἀλλὰ ῥᾳδίως, ὡς)περ SCHN. I τηκομένου
OM. SCHN. II 593 FORT. ἐκρηγνύμενος SCHN. IV 703    3. τὰ
μὲν γὰρ πρὸς βορέαν καὶ νότον ⟨ὀρεινὰ, τὰ⟩ FURL. 65,SCHN.
I E PROB. 26,52,WI.    5. οὐδὲ ὄρος οὐδὲ γῆ MAR.VAS.    6.
ὥστε MAR.VAS. E PROB. 26,52

41. And for this reason it is also steady. For it does
not blow from mountains nor from snow melted rapidly but
flows gently as through a pipe. Places to the north and
south are mountainous while to the west there is neither
mountain nor land, only the Atlantic Ocean, so that this
wind moves in upon the land. The breeze occurs in the
afternoon because of the location. All winds rise with
the sun, which scatters the moisture, or vaporizes it
and contributes to their creation. When then the sun
reaches the place, the breeze commences. During the
night it ceases because the impulse of the sun is absent.

42. This wind drives great clouds because it blows from
the Atlantic over the Mediterranean, so that it gathers
them over a long way. It is stormy and ill-blowing from
the reasons already given. For it blows after winter
while the air is still cold. Now the west wind of late
fall is not like that, unless we consider it stormy be-

WI. ⟨δὲ⟩ FURL. 65    7. γὰρ πνεύματα⟩ BON.    8. καὶ συν.
BON.    9. πνοὴ ⟨γίνεται⟩ BON. ⟨ἄρχεται⟩ HEINS.    10. ἐκ-
λείπειν BON.,SCHN. IV 703

42.    1. ὅτε ἐξ EIORU ὅτ' ἐκ CETT. ALD. ὅτι SCHN. I    2.
κατὰ τὸ ἔλαττον M κατ' ἔλαττον CETT. κατὰ θάλατταν MAR.VAS.
FORT. παρὰ θάλ. SCHN. II 593 ἐκ προπολλοῦ MSS. ἐκ πολλοῦ
MAR.VAS.,FURL. 65    3. διόπερ τὰ MSS. διότι κατὰ τὰ VEL τὸ
πρότερον MAR.VAS. διὰ τὸ ὅπερ πρότερον εἴρηται BON. διά
τε τὰ SCHN. I [τὰ] WI. πρότερον MAR.VAS. πρότερα MSS. μετὰ
δὲ DEOPQRUXZ ALD. δὲ OM. CETT. FURL. 65 μετά τε HEINS. μετὰ γὰρ WI. πνεῖν MSS. πνεῖ SCHN. I καὶ τὸ μετά τὸν χειμῶνα
πνεῖν SCHN. IV 704    4. πνέοντος $Q_1$ ῥέοντος $Q_2$ CETT. ὄντος
TURN.,MAR.VAS. ἔπειθ' MSS. ἐπεί τε BON. ἐπεὶ TURN.    5.
λαμβάνοντος XZ λαμβάνοντες CETT. λαμβάνοι τις TURN.,MAR.
VAS. λαμβάνομεν SCHN. I    6. εἰ γὰρ MSS. καὶ γὰρ FURL.

ἐν γὰρ τοῖς συνεχέσι τόποις μέγας πνεῖ, καθάπερ καὶ οἱ ἄλλοι. καὶ ληπτέον ἴσως οὕτω τὸ χειμέριον, οὐχ ὡς πᾶσιν· εἰ
μὴ ἄρα καὶ παραλλάττοντες καὶ ποιοῦνται τὴν προσηγορίαν
τὸν θρασκίαν ζέφυρον καλοῦντες· χειμέριος γὰρ οὗτος. ἀλλὰ
ταῦτα μὲν ἐπισκεπτέον.

43.  ἡ δ᾽ ὁμαλότης καὶ λειότης, ὅταν ᾖ, ποιεῖ τινα χάριν
κατὰ τὴν κίνησιν καὶ φορὰν ὥσθ᾽ ὅπου τοιοῦτος, ἐνταῦθα καὶ
ἡδύς. [εἰ μὴ ἄρα...ἐπισκεπτέον] ὅτι δὲ καὶ τοὺς καρποὺς
τοὺς μὲν φθείρει, τοὺς δὲ τρέφει, καθόλου μὲν ἐκεῖνο ἀληθὲς εἰπεῖν, ὃ καὶ κατὰ τῶν ἄλλων κοινὸν ὅτι τρέφει μὲν,
ὅπου ψυχρὸς πνεῖ τοῦ θέρους, ἀπόλλυσι δὲ ὅπου θερμὸς καὶ
πάλιν τοῦ χειμῶνος καὶ τοῦ ἦρος ὁμοίως, ὅπου μὲν ψυχρὸς,
ἀπόλλυσιν, ὅπου δὲ θερμὸς τρέφει καὶ σώζει, ἐναντίαν ταῖς
ὥραις τὴν πνοὴν ἔχων. τοῦτο δ᾽ ἐστιν, ὅταν ἐκ θαλάττης ᾖ·
θερμὴ γὰρ αὕτη χειμῶνος, θέρους δὲ ψυχρά. διὰ το  ο δὲ καὶ
ὁ νότος ἐνιαχοῦ τοιοῦτος, ὥσπερ καὶ ἐν Ἄργει. καὶ ὁ Βορ-
εᾶς δὲ παρ᾽ ἄλλοις.

44.  τὸ μὲν οὖν ἁπλοῦν καὶ κοινὸν, ὥσπερ ἐλέχθη, τοῦτο.τὰ
δὲ καθ᾽ ἑκάστους τόπους ἐκ τῆς θέσεως δεῖ καὶ τῶν ἄλλων
τῶν συμβαινόντων ἀνασκοπεῖν καὶ θεωρεῖν·εὑρήσεις γὰρ σχεδὸν ἐν ταύταις ταῖς αἰτίαις τὴν διαφοράν. οἷον τῆς Ἰταλ-
ίας ἡ μὲν ⟨Λο⟩κρὶς καὶ ἡ ταύτῃ συνεχὴς εὐθενεῖ τῷ ζεφύρῳ,

66. ἐν γὰρ SCHN. I   7. ἴσως δ᾽ ὡς MSS. οὕτω τὸ TURN. ἴσως
ὅτι ὡς FURL. 66 οὕτω SCHN. I ὡς οὐ πᾶσι MSS. οὐ DEL. BON.
SUBAUD. κοινὸν οὐ πᾶσιν ὁμοίως FURL. 66 οὐχ ὡς πᾶσιν SCHN.
I   7-10. ⟨εἰς⟩ (εἰ EIOR) μὴ ἄρα καὶ παραλᾶττον (παραλάττ-
των LM₂ ALD.) ἐστιν ἐμποιοῦνται (ἐκπ. D) τὴν προσηγορίαν
τὸν κίον ζέφυρον καλοῦντες, χειμέριος γὰρ οὗτος·ἀλλὰ ταῦτα μὲν ἐπισκεπτέον E SECT. 43⟩ SCHN. I  8.παραλάττων
FURL. 66   9. θρασκίαν ζέφυρον TURN. ὅθεν καὶ ἐμποιοῦνται
BON. χιονοζέφυρον καλοῦντες BON. εἰ μὴ ἄρα καὶ παραλάτ-
τοντες, καὶ ποιοῦνται τὴν προσηγορίαν κτλ. SCHN. I τινες
μεταποιοῦσι τὸν προσηγορίαν, τὸν θρασκίαν ζέφυρον καλοῦντες κτλ. SCHN. II 593
43. 2. [εἰ μὴ...ἐπισκεπτέον] SCHN. I   4. ὃὺς μὲν φθεί-

cause of its force. For it blows with force in continuous areas just like the other winds. Perhaps we must
understand the designation "stormy" in this sense, not in
the generalized meaning. That is, unless people are
changing the name and calling the north-north-west wind
the west wind. For the former is stormy. But this must
be looked into.

43. The level and gentle nature of this wind, when it
is thus, makes it pleasant in its action and movement,
so that where it is so conditioned, it is enjoyable.
As to the fact that it ruins some crops and nourishes
others, it is generally true to say, as is the case with
the other winds, that it nourishes when it blows cold in
the summer and ruins when it blows hot. The same principle applies in turn to winter and spring; whenever the
wind is cold, it is ruinous; whenever it is warm, it
nourishes and preserves, by having a current opposite in
nature to the season. This comes about when the wind is
from the sea; it is warm in winter and cold in summer.
For that reason the south wind is sometimes like this,
as in Argos, and the north wind elsewhere.

44. The common and general aspect of this wind has been
presented. The individual aspects here and there must
be studied under the light of local conditions and other
attendant circumstances. The differences will prove to

---

ρει, οὓς δὲ τρέφει MSS. τοὺς μὲν φθ., τοὺς δὲ τρ. FURL. 66
τοὺς μὲν τρ., τοὺς δὲ φθ. FURL. 97   7. οὗ χειμῶνος FURL.
66 μὲν ψυχρὸς DEIMOPQRUX μὲν OM. Z FURL. 66   8. ἐναντίως
MSS. ἐναντίων BAS., VAS. ἐναντίαν BON.,FURL. 66   9. ἔχον
BON.  FORT. θαλάττης πνέῃ SCHN. IV 705

44.   2. τύπους DEMOPQUX₁ τόπους X₂CETT.   3. ἀνακόπτειν
MSS. ἀνασκέπτειν  FURL. 98 ἀνασκοπεῖν SCHN. I θεωρεῖ FURL.

διὰ τὸ ἐκ ⟨τῆς⟩ θαλάττης προσπίπτειν· ἄλλη δέ τις οὐχ ὁμο-
ίως· ἔνιαι δὲ καὶ βλάπτονται. καὶ πάλιν τῆς Κρήτης ἡ μὲν
Γορτύνη τρέφεται. κεῖται γὰρ ἀναπεπτεμένη, καὶ προσβάλλει
αὐτῇ ἐκ τοῦ πελάγους. ἑτέρα δέ τις ἀπόλλυται, πρὸς 'ἣν ἐκ
τῆς γῆς καὶ ὀρῶν τινων προσπίπτει.

45. φθείρει δὲ καὶ τὰ ἐν τῷ Μαλιακῷ κόλπῳ πάντα καὶ τὰ
ἐφέτεια καὶ τὰ τῶν δένδρων, ⟨καὶ⟩ τὰ τῆς Θετταλίας περὶ
τὸν Πιέριον· ἀμφοτέρων δὲ τῶν τόπων ἡ αὐτὴ φύσις, καὶ τὰ
περιέχοντα ὅμοια. κεῖνται μὲν γὰρ ἄμφω πρὸς ἀνατολήν, περι-
έχονται δ' ὄρεσιν ὑψηλοῖς, ὁ μὲν τῇ Οἴτῃ καὶ τοῖς συνεχέσιν, ⟨ὁ δὲ τῷ Πιέρῳ⟩. ὁ δὲ ζέφυρος πνέων ἀπὸ δυσμῆς ἰσημε-
ρινῆς τὴν ὑπὸ τοῦ ἡλίου θερμότητα προσπίπτουσαν τοῖς ὄρεσιν, ἀνακλωμένην ⟨δὲ⟩ κατὰ τὴν ⟨γῆν καθῆκε⟩ εὐθὺς εἰς ⟨τὸ⟩
πεδίον καὶ ἀπέκαυσεν. ὁμοίως δὲ καὶ παρὰ τοῖς ἄλλοις, οἷς
τι τοιοῦτον 'ἢ παραπλήσιον τούτῳ συμβαῖνόν ἐστι, καὶ τοῖς
ἐναντίοις ἀνάπαλιν.

---

98  4. ἡ μὲν κρὶς D κρίσις LMPUXZ ALD. κρηὶς EIOQR λοκρὶς
TURN.,MAR.VAS. κρότων FURL. 66  5. ταῦτα MSS. ταύτῃ TURN.
FURL. 66 ἐνθέρει M εὐθένει XZ ἐνθείνει L ALD. ἐνθένει
CETT. εὐθηνεῖ MAR.VAS.,SCHN. I εὐθενεῖ EGO ἐν θαλάττης DE
IOPQRU ἐκ θ. CETT. ⟨τῆς⟩ θ. WI.  6. ἡ δ'ἄλλη  οὐχ ὁμοίως
SCHN. IV 705  7. βλάπτοντες MSS. βλάπτονται TURN.,FURL.
66 κρίους D κρίτης IOPQRUXZ κρήτης LM ALD.,FURL. 66 γορτ-
ῦνα L ALD.,FURL. 66 κορτύνα CETT. ἡ περὶ γορτύναν TURN. ἡ
μὲν περὶ γορτύνα MAR.VAS. Γορτύνη SCHN. I   8. προβάλει
τὴν IOU προσβάλλει τὴν CETT. προσβάλλει αὐτῇ MAR.VAS.,WI.
προσβάλλει πρὸς αὐτὴν SCHN. I   9. πόλλυται MZ πόλλυτα
CETT. ἀπόλλυται FURL. 66,SCHN. I

45.  1. μὴ κόλπῳ MSS. μαλακῷ κόλπῳ TURN.,FURL. 66 μαλακῷ
WI. τὰ ἐφέτια MSS. τὰ ἐπέτεια TURN.,SCHN. I ἐφέτεια EGO
2. δένδρων τὰ τῆς MSS. ⟨καὶ⟩ MAR.VAS.,FURL. 66 DEL. SCHN.
II 593 [τὰ] SCHN. I   3. τὸν κιέριον DLXZ ALD. τὸ κιέριον

lie more or less in such considerations as the following:
for example, in Locris in Italy and the neighboring territory the west wind brings fertility because it comes
from the sea. Another district is not so fortunate, and
some districts even suffer harm. The district of Gortyna
in Crete in turn is fertile, for it is open, and the west
wind reaches it from the sea. Some other region, visited
by this wind from the land and some mountains, is deso-
late.

45. In the Malic Gulf this wind destroys all growth,
both the annuals and the fruit of trees, and so too in
Thessaly near the Pierian Gulf. The lay of the land in
both cases is the same, so too the environs. Both are
open to the east and are walled off by high mountains,
the Malic Gulf by Oeta and the adjoining ranges, the
Pierian by Mt. Pierus. The west wind, blowing from equinoctial sundown, takes the heat from the sun, which has
fallen on the mountains, and deflecting it earthwards,
launches it straight into the plain and scorches it. It
is the same for other regions where this or its like occurs, and conversely with opposite situations.

---

CETT. τὸν πιέριον FURL. 66   4. περιόνθ' DIPQRU περιέχοντα LXZ FURL. 67   6. ⟨ὁ δ' 'Ολύμπῳ⟩ TURN. ⟨ὁ δὲ πιερίῳ⟩
BON. ⟨ὁ δὲ τῷ πιέρῳ⟩ SCHN. I ὁ δὲ πνέων ζέφυρος MSS. ὁ δὲ
Ζ. πν. SCHN. I   8. ἀνακλωμένην καὶ τὴν LAC. 17 LITT. εὐθὺς MSS. ἀνακλωμένην καθεῖκε εἰς MAR.VAS. ἀνακλωμένην δὲ
⟨ἀποπέμπει⟩ FURL. 68,SCHN. I FORT. ἀνα. τε SCHN. II 594
ἀνακλωμένην ἐξέτραπεν εὐθὺς εἰς τὸ πεδίον WI. εἰς πεδίον
κατέπεσεν STEIN. 49 κατὰ τὴν ⟨γῆν καθεῖκε⟩ EGO [ἀποπεμπει]
SCHN. IV 706 εἰς ⟨τὸ⟩ FURL. 67,SCHN. I   9. ταῖς ἄλλαις Ζ
αἷς εἴτε EIOR αἷς εἴ τι τοιοῦτον CETT. οἷς τι τοι. TURN.,
MAR.VAS. ὅπου τι τοιοῦτον SCHN. IV 706   10. τοῦτο MSS.
τούτῳ SCHN. I

46. ὅλως γὰρ, ὃ πολλάκις λεγεται, τοῦτ᾽ἀληθές, ὅτι μέγα
συμβάλλεται δι᾽ὧν ᾽ἂν πνέῃ καὶ ὅθεν εἴς τε τἆλλα καὶ εἰς
θερμότητα καὶ εἰς ψυχρότητα. διὰ τοῦτο γὰρ καὶ ὁ νότος
ψυχρός, οὐχ ἧττον τοῦ βορέου κατὰ τὴν παροιμίαν, ὅτι ⟨διὰ
τὸν⟩ ἀέρα κατεψυγμένον ἔτι καὶ ὑγρὸν ὑπὸ τοῦ χειμῶνος τοιαύτην ἀνάγκη τὴν πνοὴν προσπίπτειν, οἷος ᾽ἂν ὁ ἀὴρ ᾖ.ὁ δὲ
βορέας ὁ ἐπὶ τὸν πηλὸν τῶν νότων, ὅν φησι πάλιν ἡ παροιμία
χειμῶνα ποιεῖν, διὰ τὴν αὐτὴν αἰτίαν ποιεῖ. βρεχθεὶς γὰρ
ὁ ἀὴρ ψυχρός. ὡσαύτως δὲ καὶ ⟨αἱ⟩ ἀπὸ τῶν ποταμῶν, ὥσπερ
ἐλέχθη πρότερον.

47. ἡ μὲν ⟨οὖν⟩ τούτων ἰδιότης ἔχει τινὰ λόγον. ὅτι δὲ
τὰ πνεύματα τοῦ μὲν χειμῶνος καὶ τοῦ ἑωθινοῦ ἀπὸ τῆς ἕω
πνεῖ, τοῦ δὲ θέρους καὶ τῆς δείλης ἀπὸ τῆς ἑσπέρας, ἐκείνην τὴν αἰτίαν ὑποληπτέον, ⟨ὅτι⟩ ὅταν ὁ ἥλιος ἕλκων μηκέτι
κρατῇ, τότε ἀφιέμενος ὁ ἀὴρ ῥεῖ, καὶ δυόμενος. οὖν καταλείπει νέφη, ἀφ᾽ ὧν τὰ ζεφύρια. καὶ ὅσον ᾽ἂν ἐπάγῃ τοῖς ἐν τῷ
κάτω ἡμισφαιρίῳ κατοικοῦσιν ⟨ἑωθινὸν⟩ πνεῦμα γίνεται·τοῦ-
ναντίον δὲ ὅταν δύνῃ ἐν τῷ κάτω μέρει, ζεφύρους μὲν ἐκεί-

46. 1. ὅτι MSS.,WI. ὅτε SCHN. I   2. ἀναπνέει L ALD. ἀν-
απνέῃ CETT. ᾽ἂν πνέῃ TURN.,MAR.VAS.   5. ⟨διὰ τὸν⟩ TURN.,
MAR.VAS. ⟨διὰ⟩ FURL. 67   6. ἀνάγκη L ALD.,FURL. 67 ἀνάγην
Z ἀνάγκην CETT. ἀναπνοὴν MSS. πνοὴν TURN.,MAR.VAS. ἥν MSS.
ᾖ MAR.VAS.,SCHN. I καὶ βορέας MSS. ὁ δὲ βορέας ὁ SCHN. I
7. τῶν ὄντων MSS. τῶν νότων MAR.VAS.,DEL. FURL. 67, SCHN.
I τὸ δ᾽ ἐπὶ τὸν πηλὸν τὸν νότον BON.   8. αἰτίαν ποιεῖ
FURL. 67   9. καὶ αἱ M αἱ OM. CETT. δὲ καὶ αἱ EGO

47. 1. ⟨οὖν⟩ SCHN. I τὸν εὔλογον D τιν᾽ εὔλογον CETT.
τινὰ λόγον TURN.,MAR.VAS.   2. τὸ ἑωθινὸν MSS. τοῦ ἑωθινοῦ
FURL. 67,SCHN. I   4. ⟨ὅτι⟩ FURL. 99 OM. MSS.,WI. κρατεῖν
MSS. κρατῇ MAR.VAS.,SCHN. I δύναται⟩ FURL. 67   5. κρατεῖ
ἀφιέμενος ὁ ἀὴρ FURL. 99 ποτ᾽ ἀφιέμενος MSS. τότε ἀφιέμενος BON. ὁ ἀὴρ εἰσδυόμενος MSS. ὁ ἀὴρ ῥεῖ MAR.VAS. ⟨καὶ⟩
δυόμενος SCHN. I ὁ ἀὴρ καὶ εἰσδυόμ. FURL. 67 ⟨οὖν⟩ SCHN.

46. In general, the frequently made statement holds
true, that it makes a great difference through what
areas and from what areas a wind passes, both with regard to other matters and with regard to temperature.
For this reason the south wind also is cold, no less
than the north wind, as is stated in the proverb, because, with the air still cooled and moistened by the
winter, the wind must arrive in the same condition as
the air. The north wind which comes upon the mud of
the south wind, which the proverb again says makes
stormy weather, does so for the same reason. For air
which is humidified is cold. And so it is with breezes
from rivers, as has been already stated.

47. The individual character of the winds has a reasonable explanation. The reason why winds blow from the
east in winter and at dawn, but from the west in summer
and in the afternoon must be considered to be the following: when the sun draws air but no longer controls
it, the air is released and flows, and when the sun
sinks, it leaves behind clouds, from which the west
winds are derived. Whatever material the sun carries
with it becomes the morning wind for those who live in
the western hemisphere; conversely, when the sun sinks

II 594 συγκαλύπτει MSS. ἐκλείπει BON. συγκαταλείπει SCHN.
I [καὶ] δυόμενος οὖν καταλείπει WI. ⟨νέφη⟩ FURL. 67 ἀφ'οὗ
MSS. ἀφ' ὧν FURL. 67 ὅσον ἀνάγει MSS. ὅσον 'ἂν ἐπάγῃ SCHN.
I ἄγῃ SCHN. II 594 ὅσον 'ἂν ἄγῃ WI.   7. ⟨κάτω⟩ BON.,FURL.
67 κάτω πρὸς τὸ ἡμέτερον STEIN. 50 κατοικοῦσι LAC. 13
LITT. πνεῦμα MSS. ἑωθινὸν πνεῦμα MAR.VAS.,SCHN. I κατινάτι
L κατενάντι CETT. ALD. τοὐναντίον MAR.VAS.,SCHN. I τἀναν-
τία FURL. 67   8. δύηται MSS. δύνῃ FURL. 67,SCHN. I μερίζεται θέρους MSS. μέρει ζεφύρους MAR.VAS.,SCHN. I μέρει ζεφύροις FURL. 67 ζεφύροις ἐκείνοις HEINS.   9. τὸ δ' ἐντεῦθεν MSS. τὸ δ' ἐνταῦθα BON. τοῖς δ' ἐνταῦθα FURL. 67

νοις ποιήσει, τοῖς δ' ἐνταῦθα ἑωθινὸν πνεῦμα, ἀπὸ τοῦ συν-
επομένου ἀέρος αὐτῷ.

48.  διὰ τοῦτο καὶ ἐὰν λάβῃ πνέοντα ἄλλον ἄνεμον, μείζων
γίνεται, διότι προσέθηκεν. ὥσπερ ⟨δὲ⟩ ὁ ζέφυρος ἀεὶ καὶ
πόρρω πνεῖ τοῖς ἑσπερίοις, οὕτω τοῖς κάτω πρὸς τὴν ἡμετέραν ἕω, ἐκείνη δ' ἑσπέραν, ἄλλα πνεύματα. ταῦτα μὲν οὖν
παρὰ τὴν ὁμοιότητα παρ' ἑκατέροις, ἥ τε ⟨ἐν⟩ τοῖς ἄκροις
ἑκάστων πνοὴ γίνεται μὲν ὥσπερ καὶ τὰ ὕδατα καὶ τὰ ἄλλα
κατὰ συμβεβηκός· οὐ μήν γε κατ' ἀκρίβειαν, ἀλλ' ὡς ἐπὶ τὸ
πᾶν. εἴωθε δὲ ὥσπερ ἄλλο τι τῶν τεταγμένων καὶ ἐπὶ τῷ κυνὶ
ὁ νότος πνεῖν. αἴτιον δὲ ὅτι θερμὰ τὰ κάτω τοῦ ἡλίου ⟨οὐ⟩
πόρρω ὄντος, ὥστε γίνεται πολλὴ ἀτμίς. ἔπνεον δ' ἂν πολλοὶ μὴ κωλυόμενοι τοῖς ἐτησίαις. νῦν δ' οὗτοι διακωλύουσιν.

49.  οἱ δὲ νυκτερινοὶ βορέαι τριταῖοι πίπτουσιν· ὅθεν ἡ
παροιμία λέγεται ὡς οὔποτε νυκτερινὸς βορέας τρίτον ἵκετο
φέγγος, διότι ἀσθενῆ τὰ πνεύματα γίνεται τὰ ἀπὸ τῆς ἄρκτου
νύκτωρ ἀρξάμενα. φανερὸν γάρ, ὡς ⟨οὐ⟩ πολὺς ὁ κινηθεὶς
ἀὴρ, ὅταν τηνικαῦτα πνέῃ, τῆς θερμότητος ὀλίγης οὔσης· ὀλίγον γὰρ ὀλίγη κινεῖ. τελευτᾷ δὲ πάντα ἐν τρίσιν, καὶ τὰ
ἐλάχιστα δ' ἐν τῇ πρώτῃ τριάδι. ὅτι δ' οὐκ αὐτὸ τοῦτο συμβαίνει καὶ ἐπὶ τοῦ νότου νυκτερινοῦ πνεύσαντος, αἴτιον,
ὅτι ἐγγὺς ὁ ἥλιός ἐστι τῆς πρὸς νότον χώρας, καὶ ἀλεεινό-
τεραι αἱ νύκτες ἐκεῖ 'ἡ πρὸς ἄρκτον αἱ ἡμέραι. καὶ ⟨πολὺς⟩

48.  1. τούτῳ MSS. διὰ τοῦτο FURL. 67, SCHN. I ἄνεμον ὡς
μὲν οὐ μείζω L ALD. 'ὸς CETT. οὐ DEL. BON. ἄνεμον μείζων
FURL. 67, SCHN. I οὗτος μὲν οὖν μείζων γίνεται διότι προσ.
SCHN. II 594   2. ⟨δὲ⟩ TURN., MAR.VAS.   3. οὕτω ⟨καὶ⟩ BON.
4. ⌊ἄλλα πνεύματα⌋ BON. ⟨διὰ ταῦτα⟩ BON.   5. ⟨ἐν⟩ SCHN.I
7. γὰρ ἀκρείβειαν L ALD. γ' ἀκρίβιαν U γ' ἀκρίβειαν CETT.
δι' ἀκρίβειαν BON. γε ⟨κατ'⟩ ἀκρ. FURL. 67, SCHN. I ἔωθεν
MSS. εἴωθε SCHN. I τόδε ὥσπερ BON. τῆς τεταγμένης MSS. τῶν
τεταγμένων MAR.VAS., SCHN. I ἐπὶ κοινηνότε MSS. ἐκείνην ὅτε
MAR.VAS. ἐπὶ κυνὶ τὸν νότον BON. ἐπὶ κοινοῖς FURL. 67 ἐπὶ

in the western hemisphere, it produces west winds there,
while for us here it produces a morning wind from the
air which accompanies it.

48. For this reason, if a wind picks up another wind,
it becomes stronger by the addition. Just as the west
wind is always blowing far in the west, so for those in
the western hemisphere other winds blow toward our dawn,
their sundown. This happens in each case by parallelism, and the breeze takes place at the extreme times in
each hemisphere, not in exact pattern but in a general
way. The south wind blows, like any other of the regular winds, when Sirius rises. The reason is that the
southern areas are hot because the sun is not far off,
so that much vapor is produced. The south wind would
blow frequently if the etesians did not interfere, but
in fact they do.

49. North winds coming at night drop away in three
days. From this is derived the proverb: never does the
nocturnal north wind see the third day. Reason: winds
from the north beginning at night are weak. For it is
clear that the air set in motion is not great in amount
when it blows at that time, since the heat is limited.
For little heat moves little air. They all end in three
days, and the weakest on the first day. The reason that
this does not happen to the south wind when it blows at
night is that the sun is near the region to the south,

τῷ κυνὶ [ὸ νότος] αἴτιον [δὲ] FURL. 67 FORT. [αἴτιον]
SCHN. IV 708    9. πόρρω ὄντος MSS. παρόντος FURL. 67,
SCHN. I ἡλίου ⟨οὐ⟩ πόρρω ὄντος SCHN. IV 162    10. δ' ἐησ-
ίας DEMRUX₁ δ' ἐκσίαις I ἐτησίαις L ALD. δ'ἐτησίαις PQX₃Z
49.  2. καὶ τὸ φέγγος MSS. ἵκετο TURN.,MAR.VAS    4. φαν-
ερὰ φανερὸν MAR.VAS.,FURL. 68 ὡς ⟨οὐ⟩ FURL. 68,SCHN. I  5.
ὀλίγον γὰρ ἀέρα θερμότης κινεῖ MAR.VAS.    7. τριάδι ⟨ἡ
τρίτη δὲ κρίσιμος⟩ SCHN. V,LVII    10.'ἡ OM. FURL. 68 ἄρκ-

ὁ κινούμενος ἀὴρ [καὶ] οὐδὲν ἔλαττον 'ἦν μεθ'ἡμέραν.ἀλλ'
ὅσῳ θερμότεραι αἱ ἡμέραι, κωλύουσι ⟨μᾶλλον⟩ πνεῖν ξηραίνουσαι τὰς ὑγρότητας.

50. τάχα δ' κἀκεῖνο τοῦ βορέου ⟨αἴτιον⟩ ὅτι ἀθρόως ἡ ἔκχυσις, ὥσπερ τῶν ἐκνεφίων· ταχεῖα δ' ἡ παῦλα τῶν ἀθρόων.
⟨ἀπ'⟩ ἀσθενοῦς ⟨δ'⟩ ἀρχῆς ⟨οὐ πολὺ⟩ τὸ μέγεθος. ἀεὶ δ'ὡς
ἐπίπαν λάβρος, μετὰ ⟨δὲ⟩ χιόνα καὶ πάχνην ⟨νότος⟩. ὅθεν
καὶ ἡ παροιμία· φιλεῖ δὲ νότος μετὰ πάχνην, ὅτι πέψεώς τινος γινομένης καὶ ἀποκαθάρσεως, ἑκάτερόν τι πίπτει.μετὰ δὲ
τὴν πέψιν καὶ τὴν ἀποκάθαρσιν εἰς τοὐναντίον ἡ μεταβολή·
βορέᾳ δ' ἐναντίος ὁ νότος. δι' αὐτὸ τοῦτο καὶ μετὰ τὸν
ὑετὸν καὶ τὴν χάλαζαν καὶ τὰς τοιαύτας τινὰς ⟨ἀποκαθάρ-
σεις⟩ ὡς ἐπὶ τὸ πολὺ πίπτει τὰ πνεύματα. πάντα γὰρ ταῦτα
καὶ τὰ τοιαῦτα πέψεις καὶ ἀποκαθάρσεις τινές εἰσιν.

51. ἐπεὶ δὲ πρὸς τὰς χώρας ἑκάστοις καὶ τοὺς τόπους ἐπί-
νεφῆ καὶ αἴθρίαι, διὰ τοῦτο καὶ τῶν ἐν παροιμίᾳ λεγομένων
πρός τινας τόπους ἔνια, ὡς περὶ τοῦ ἀργέστου καὶ λιβός.
ἰσχυρὸς δὲ μάλιστα περὶ Κνίδον καὶ 'Ρόδον 'ὢν, λὶψ ἄνεμος

τὸν δὲ ἡμέραι ὁ κινούμενος ἀὴρ MSS. ἄρκτον αἱ ἡμέραι FURL.
68,SCHN. I καὶ ⟨πολὺς⟩ SCHN. I    11. ἀὴρ καὶ οὐδὲν MSS.
[καὶ] MAR.VAS. ἐλάττων L ALD.,FURL. 68    12. κωλύουσι
⟨μᾶλλον⟩ SCHN. I OM. MSS.,WI. ἐξηραίνουσι DXZ ξηραίνουσι
CETT. [αἱ] ξηραίνουσι BAS. ξηραίνουσαι SCHN. I

50.   1. κἀκείνου MSS. κἀκείνων FURL. 100 βορέου LAC. 18
LITT. MSS. ⟨αἴτιον⟩ FURL. 68,SCHN. I ἔγχυσις MSS. ἔκχυσις
BON.,SCHN. I   2. ἐκνεφίων LAC. 10 LITT. ταχεῖα MSS. ⟨πνο-
ὴν⟩ BON.   3. ⟨δὲ⟩ ἀρχῆς FURL. 68 ἀπ' ἀσθενοῦς δ'ἀρχῆς οὐ
πολὺ τὸ μέγεθος SCHN. II 595 οὐδὲν WI. ἀσθενοῦς δ' ἀπ' ἀρχῆς ⟨οὐ πολὺ⟩ τὸ μέγεθος·ἀεὶ δ' ὡς ἐπίπαν λάβρος ⟨ὁ βορ-
έας⟩ μετὰ ⟨δὲ⟩ χιόνα καὶ πάχνην ⟨ὁ νότος⟩ πνεῖ SCHN. V,
LVII   4. λαῦρος MSS. λάβρος TURN.,SCHN. I λαμπρὸς BON.
AQUILO  TURN. ⟨ὁ νότος⟩ MAR.VAS. ⟨βορέας⟩ SCHN. II 595 μετὰ δὲ χιόνα MSS. δὲ OM. SCHN. I μετὰ δὲ χιόνα καὶ πάχνην
WI.   5. φιλεῖ δὲ νότος MSS. καὶ πάχνην πνεῖ νότος MAR.VAS.

and the nights there are warmer than the days in the
north, and the amount of air set in motion is no less
than by day. Whereas the hotter the days, the more they
prevent wind by drying up the moisture.

50. Perhaps this too is a reason for the north wind's
behavior, that it breaks forth in concentration like a
hurricane. The cessation of concentrated winds is rapid;
out of a weak source no great force emerges. The north
wind is almost always strong, while the south wind is
strong after snow and frost, whence the proverb: south
wind likes to blow after frost. For when a concoction
and the purification occur, the change is to the opposite, and the south wind is the opposite of the north
wind. Because of this the winds generally occur after
rain, hail, and such purifications. All these and the
like are kinds of concoction and purification of the
air.

51. Since fair weather and clouds are associated with
each wind according to the district and the local area,
some of the things said in proverbs apply to certain
places, as for example the west-north-west and the west-
south-west winds. The west-south-west wind, which is
forceful near Cnidos and Rhodes makes clouds quickly and

---

πνεῖ ὁ νότος BON. ὁ νότος πνεῖ SCHN. II 595 ⟨μέγα⟩ μετὰ
MAR.VAS.   6. [τι] πνεῦμα INTELLEGENDUM SCHN. II 595     8.
τὸ αὐτὸ τοῦτο WI. ὅτι μετὰ MSS.,WI. καὶ μετὰ FURL. 68    9.
τινὰς OM. WI. ⟨χειμασίας⟩ FURL. 68 ἀποκαθάρσεις E PROB.
26,3 EGO παχὺ MSS. πολὺ MAR.VAS.

51.  2. ⟨τὰ⟩ τῶν FURL. 68, OM. WI.   3. τόπους εἰσὶν MSS.
τόπους ἔνια WI. ὥσπερ MSS. ὡς τὰ περὶ TURN.,MAR.VAS. ὥστε
BON. [τὰ] SCHN. I διὰ τοῦτο καὶ τῶν ἐν παροιμίᾳ λεγομένων
πρός τινας τόπους εἰσὶν ὥσπερ STEIN. 51 λιβὸς ᾗ χρῶνται
TURN.,WI. λιβὸς χρῶνται BON.   4. αἰσχρὸν MSS. ἰσχυρὸς

ταχὺ μὲν νεφέλας, ταχὺ δ' αἴθρια ποιεῖ· ἀργέστῃ δ' ἀνέμῳ
πᾶσ' ἕπεται νεφέλη. περὶ γὰρ τοὺς τόπους τούτους ὅ τε λὶψ
ἀμφότερα ταχέως ποιεῖ, πνέων ἀπὸ τοιαύτης ἀρχῆς· ὁ δ' ἀργέστης ταχὺ δασύνει τὸν οὐρανόν.

52. ἐνιαχοῦ δὲ καθάπερ τάξις τίς ἐστι τῶν πνευμάτων, ὥς-
τε θάτερον μετὰ θάτερον πνεῖν, ἐὰν μένῃ τινὰ χρόνον. τάχα
δὲ οὐδὲ τὸ ὅλον ἄτοπον τό γετοιοῦτο,εἴπερ ἡ περίστασις ἀεὶ
τῶν ἀνέμων εἰς τοὺς ἐφεξῆς καὶ πάλιν μεταβολὴ εἰς τοὺς ἐν-
αντίους.δύο γὰρ οὗτοι τρόποι μεταλλαγῆς 'ἢ περιισταμένων 'ἢ
ἐκπνευσάντων τελέως.ὧν ἡ μὲν κατὰ τὴν περίστασίν ⟨ἐστι⟩
εἰς τοὺς ἐφεξῆς. (ἐγγυτάτω γὰρ αὕτη ⟨ἡ⟩ μετάβασις, ἐν ᾗ
καὶ ἀναστρέφει πολλάκις ἐπὶ τὸν αὐτόν, ὅταν ὑπὸ χειμῶνος
ἀοριστία τις ᾖ), ἡ δὲ κατὰ τὴν μεταβολὴν εἰς τοὺς ἐναντί-
ους.

53. καὶ ὅλως οὕτω πέφυκεν ἐπὶ πάντων καὶ ἐπὶ τούτων ἡ
ἀνταπόδοσις καὶ οἷον ἡ ἀντίρροια κατὰ λόγον. ὁ περὶ τὰς
ἀπογαίας ὑπάρχει πρὸς τὰς τροπαίας·αὕτη δὲ πολλαχοῦ καθάπερ ἐφήμερός ἐστι τάξις τῆς μεταβολῆς. ἐνιαχοῦ δ' οὐ
τροπαία τὸ ἀντιπνέον, ἀλλ' ἕτερόν τι πνεῦμα πελάγιον

FURL. 68 κίνδον DEIMOPQRUXZ κνίδον L ALD. περὶ κνίδον
⟨γὰρ⟩ καὶ ῥόδον BON. ⟨ὧν⟩ EGO 5. ταχὺ δὲ νεφέλη DEIOQRUXZ
νεφέλην P νεφέλας LM ALD. ταχὺ μὲν νεφέλας BON. E VERS.
TURN.,SCHN. 1 τάχα μὲν αἰθίας L ALD. αἴθρια U,SCHN. I αἴ-
θριαι CETT. αἰθρίαν FURL. 68  6. πάνθ' ἕπεται WOOD-SYMONS
τούτοις CAM. 7. ὅ τ' ἀργέστης MSS. ὁ δ' ἀργέστης SCHN. I

52.  2. μένῃ MSS. καὶ μένειν BON. μείνῃ SCHN. II 596 ὅλως
BON. 3. τοιοῦτοι CAM  4. μεταβολὴν MSS. καὶ πάλιν μεταβολὴ MAR.VAS.,BON. μεταβάλλειν FURL. 69 μεταβάλλει FURL.
101 5. εἴπερ ἱσταμένων MSS. 'ἢ περιισταμένων BON. μεταλλαγῆς ὧν ἡ κατὰ τὴν περίστασιν κατ' εὖρος εἰς τοὺς ἐφεξῆς
περιισταμένων καὶ τελέως ἐκπνευσάντων SCHN. II 597  6.
εὖρος εἰς MSS. περίστασιν εἰς τὸ ἐγγύς, οἷον εὔρου εἰς
τοὺς ἐφεξῆς TURN. ⟨ἐκρέει⟩ εἰς FURL. 69 ⟨ἐστι⟩ EGO  7.

makes fair weather quickly, while every cloud follows
the west-north-west wind; for near these islands the
west-south-west wind creates both conditions rapidly,
blowing from the origin it does, while the west-north-
west wind quickly darkens the sky.

52. In some places there is something like a succession of the winds, so that one follows another if the
wind continues a length of time. This hypothesis may
not be wholly mistaken if there is a circular movement
of the winds to the next wind and on the other hand a
change to the opposite wind. For there are these two
ways of shifting, circular movement and exhaustion.
The first change takes place by the circular movement
to the next wind (this transfer is the closest; during
it there is frequently a shift back to the original
when there is a certain aimlessness caused by the
storm); the second occurs through a shift to the opposite wind.

53. In general the reciprocal action in all cases and
in these cases especially, and a sort of counterflow,
occur logically. This is true of the off-land winds
in relation to the reversing winds. In many places
this is a kind of daily order of alternation, as it

---

⟨ἡ⟩ SCHN. II 597    8. ἀντανατρέφει DEIMOPQRUXZ ἀναστρέφει
L ALD.,FURL. 69 τῶν αὐτῶν MSS. τὸν αὐτὸν SCHN. I E VERS.
TURN. ὁ ἀρκτιά τις DLXZ ALD. ἀρκτιάτης CETT. ἀοριστία τις
ἢ TURN.,MAR.VAS.    9. η MSS. ἢ FURL. 69

53.    1. πέφηνεν MSS. πέφυκεν BON. ἀνταπόδοσις P    2. ὅπερ
καὶ τὰς MSS. καὶ OM. CAM. ὅπερ καὶ ⟨περὶ⟩ FURL. 69 ὃ καὶ
περὶ MAR.VAS. ὃ περὶ WI.    3. ὑπάρχειν MSS. πάσχειν SC.
συμβαίνει BON. ὑπάρχει SCHN. I πολλάκις BON.    4. τροπαιᾷ
D FURL. 69    5. ὥσπερ καὶ περὶ MSS. ὅπερ καὶ περὶ MAR.VAS.

ὥσπερ καὶ περὶ τὸν Παμφυλικὸν κόλπον. ἔωθεν μὲν γὰρ Ἰδυρὶς καλούμενος ἀπὸ τοῦ ποταμοῦ τοῦ Ἰδύρου πνεῖ μέγας καὶ
πολὺς ἐπιπνεῖ δ᾽ αὐτῷ νότος καὶ εὖρος. ὅταν δ᾽ ἀντικόφωσιν
ἀλλήλοις, κύματός τε μέγεθος αἴρεται, συνωθουμένης τῆς
θαλάττης, καὶ πρηστῆρες πολλοὶ πίπτουσιν, ὑφ᾽ ὧν καὶ τὰ
πλοῖα ἀπόλλυνται.

54. τὸ γὰρ ὅλον ὅπου τοιαύτη σύγκρουσις γίνεται τῶν ἀνέμων, καὶ κυμάτων μέγεθος αἴρεται καὶ χειμὼν γίνεται πολύς·
ὥσπερ ὅταν, ἀντιπνεόντων ἀλλήλοις, μάχεσθαι φῶσι τοὺς ἀνέμους. ἐπεὶ κἀκεῖνο κατὰ λόγον ἐστὶν, ὅταν ἐπιπέσωσιν ἀλλήλοις μήπω τελέως ἐκπεπνευκόσι, τὸν χειμῶνα ποιεῖν·οἷον γὰρ
ὕλην παρέθηκε θάτερος θατέρῳ. μᾶλλον δὲ τοῦτο ἐμφανὲς ἐπὶ
τοῦ βορέου. χειμεριώτερος γὰρ οὗτος, καὶ εὐθὺ τὴν προσεν-
εχθεῖσαν ⟨ὕλην⟩ ἔπηξεν. ὡσαύτως δὲ καὶ ὁ νότος ἐξύγρανε
καὶ ὑδατώδη ἐποίησεν.ἐνιαχοῦ δὲ καὶ τοὺς νιφετοὺς δοκεῖ
ποιεῖν, ὥσπερ καὶ περὶ τὸν Πόντον καὶ τὸν Ἑλλήσποντον,
ὅταν ὁ βορέας οὕτω γένηται ψυχρός, ὥστε πήξας κατέχειν·
οὐ μὴν ἀλλά γε τὸ πλεῖον διέτηξεν ἢ εἰς ὕδωρ διέλυσεν.

55. καὶ αὗται μὲν οἷον χειμεριναί τινες ἐπίπνοαι καὶ ἀν-
τικόφεις·αἱ δ᾽ ἐπ᾽Ὠρίωνος ἀνατολῇ καὶ δύσει τῶν πνευμάτων ἀκρισίαι συμβαίνουσιν, ὅτι ἐν μεταβολαῖς ἀεὶ πάντα
μάλιστα πέφυκεν ἀοριστεῖν. ὁ δ᾽Ὠρίων ἀνατέλλει μὲν ἐν
ἀρχῇ ὀπώρας, δύνει δὲ ἐν ἀρχῇ χειμῶνος. ὥστε διὰ τὸ μήπω

τὸν L ALD. OM. CETT.   6. δυρὶς MSS. ἴρις VEL λιριμὸς BON.
Ἰδυρὶς BOEKER 2340   9. μέγεθος M FURL. 69 μεγέθους CETT.

54.   5. ἐκπεπλευκόσι L ALD. ἐκπεπευκόσι CETT. ἐκπεπνευκόσι TURN.,FURL. 69   6. θατέρῳ δὲ μᾶλλον τοῦτο DEILMOPQ
RUX δὲ μᾶλλον ἐμφανὲς τοῦτο Z μᾶλλον δὲ τοῦτο MAR.VAS.
μᾶλλον δὲ τοῦτ᾽ SCHN. I   7. χειμερινώτερος L ALD.   8.
⟨ὕλην⟩ FURL. 69 τῆξιν MSS. ἔπηξεν MAR.VAS.   9. καὶ OM. L
FURL. 103   12. πλοῖον DLXZ

55.   1. καὶ ταῦτα BAS. ἀντικώφις L ἀντικώφεις CETT. ALD.
ἀντικόφεις TURN.,FURL. 69   2. ἤδη MSS. αἱ δ᾽ MAR.VAS.

were. In some places the counter-wind is not a reversing wind but another wind from the sea, as happens in the Pamphylian Gulf. At dawn the wind called Idyris blows from the River Idyros in force and volume, followed by the south wind and the east-south-east wind. When they come into conflict with each other, great waves arise, since the sea is pushed together, and many waterspouts occur, by which ships are wrecked.

54. Usually when such a collision of winds occurs, great waves are caused and a great storm arises, as when people speak of the winds fighting when they blow against each other. For it is logical that when winds encounter each other before they have blown themselves out, they should create a storm; each wind provides material for the other, so to say. This is more evident with the north wind. It is stormier and quickly freezes the material which has been added. Similarly, the south wind renders the material moist and liquid. In some places it also appears to cause snowfalls, as in the Black Sea region and the Dardanelles, when the north wind is so cold that it prevails and freezes the material. Certainly it freezes more than it melts.

55. Such are the successions and conflicts of the winds in winter, we may say. The winds which come when Orion rises and sets are of no fixed character because during transitions all phenomena are very uncertain. Orion rises at the beginning of autumn and sets at the beginning of winter, with the result that, because it does

3. ἀκρασίαι MSS. ἀκρισίαι BON. οὖ τ' ἐνι DL ALD. οὖ δ' ἐν-
ίαις CETT. ὅτι FURL. 69 E VERS. TURN. ὅτι ἐν SCHN. I   5.
μηδεμίαν MSS. WI. [μηδὲ] SCHN. I  8-10. διαταρίζειν LAC.
13 LITT. αἴακα αὐτόθι (αὐτόθη P) δὴ χαλεπὸν γίνεται καὶ
δύνων καὶ ἀνατέλλων (ἀνατέλων M) εἶναι διὰ τὴν ἀοριστίαν
τῆς ὥρας. ἀνάγκη καὶ ταραχώδη (τὰ ταραχώδη M) καὶ ἀνωμαλῆ

καθεστᾶναι μηδεμίαν ὥραν, τῆς μὲν γινομένης, τῆς δὲ παυο-
μένης, ἀνάγκη καὶ τὰ πνεύματα ἀκατάστατα καὶ ἄκριτα εἶναι,
διὰ τὸ ἐπαμφοτερίζειν τὰ ἐξ ἑκατέρας, ὅθεν δὴ καὶ χαλεπὸς
λέγεται καὶ δύνων καὶ ἀνατέλλων εἶναι, διὰ τὴν ἀοριστίαν
τῆς ὥρας. ἀνάγκη γὰρ ταραχώδη καὶ ἀνωμαλῆ εἶναι.

56.    καὶ ταῦτα μὲν οὖν καὶ ὅσα ἄλλα τοιαῦτα περὶ τὸν ἀέρα
καὶ τὸν ὅλον οὐρανὸν συμβαίνει· τὰ δὲ ⟨ἀναχθήσεται⟩ εἰς
τὰς ἡμετέρας διαθέσεις·οἷον βαρύτερον ἐν τοῖς νοτίοις ἔχ-
ουσιν ⟨οἱ⟩ ἄνθρωποι καὶ ἀδυνατώτερον. αἴτιον δὲ ὅτι ἐξ
⟨ὀλίγου⟩ πολὺ ὑγρὸν γίνεται ⟨διατηκόμενον διὰ τὴν ἀλέαν⟩
καὶ ὑγρότης βαρεῖα ἀντὶ κούφου πνεύματος. ἔτι δ' ἡ μὲν
ἰσχὺς καὶ δύναμις ἐν τοῖς ἄρθροις ἐστίν. ⟨ταῦτα δὲ ἀνίεται
ὑπὸ τῶν νοτίων. τὸ γὰρ γλίσχρον ἐν τοῖς ἄρθροις πεπηγὸς
μὲν κωλύει⟩ κινεῖσθαι ἡμᾶς, ὑγρὸν δὲ λίαν 'ὂν συμτείνεσ-
θαι. τὰ δὲ βόρεια ποιεῖ τινα συμμετρίαν, ὥστε καὶ ἰσχύειν
καὶ συντείνεσθαι.

_____

εἶναι MSS.   8. εἶναι καὶ ἀμφοτερίζειν οἷα καὶ αὐτόθι δὴ
χαλεπὸς γίνεται MAR.VAS. διὰ τὸ ἀμφοτερίζειν τὰ ἐξ ἑκατέρας καὶ χαλεπὸς δὲ λέγεται καὶ δύνων FURL. 70 διὰ τὸ παρ-
εγκλίνειν ἐφ' ἑκάτερα καὶ χαλεπὸς δὴ λέγεται SCHN. II 598
ἀπαμφοτερίζειν ἐξ ἑκατέρας, ὅθεν δὴ καὶ χαλεπὸς λέγεται
SCHN. V 162   9. ἀνατέλλων. ἔτι διὰ τὸ μέγεθος τοῦ ἄστρου.
ἐκ πολλῶν γὰρ ἀστέρων καὶ πολὺ μέρος κατέχειν. διὸ οὐ πᾶς
ἅμα οὔτε ἐπιτέλλει, ἀλλ' ἐν πολλαῖς ἡμέραις. διὸ καὶ παρα-
τείνει ὁ χειμών. SCHN. V 162

56.    1. 'ἢ ταῦτα MSS. καὶ ταῦτα FURL. 70,SCHN. I   2. τὰ
δὲ LAC. 10-20 LITT. MSS. ⟨ἀναχθήσεται⟩ BON.   3. ἕτερον
MSS. βαρύτερον MAR.VAS. νοτείοις L ALD.   4. ⟨οἱ⟩ MAR.VAS.
ἀνθρώπων MSS. ἄνθρωποι SCHN. I ἄρτιον MSS. αἴτιον MAR.VAS.
4-5. ἄρτιον δ' ὅτι ἐξ LAC. 7-19 LITT. MSS.   4. ⟨ὀλίγου⟩
MAR.VAS.,FURL. 70 πολὺ ὑγρὸν γίνεται καὶ ἡ πνεύματος ὑγρότης βορέαν (βαρέαν MQRU,βορέα XZ) ἀντὶ κούφου MSS. πολὺ
ὑγρὸν γίνεται ⟨διατηκόμενον διὰ τὴν ἀλέαν⟩ καὶ ἀντὶ κούφου

not coincide with a single season (the end of one, the
beginning of the other), the winds are necessarily unstable and uncertain, partaking of the nature of both
seasons. And so the star is called "difficult" when
rising and setting because of the unsettled character
of the season. The winds then are bound to be turbu-
lent and irregular.

56. These then and all other such things occur in the
air and throughout the sky. Other phenomena are related
to our state of being. For example, we are more slug-
gish and weaker under south winds. This is because a
little moisture is succeeded by a great deal, being
melted by the warmth, and heavy moisture succeeds a
light breeze. In addition, strength and power are located in our joints. These become slack under the influence of the south wind; the viscous fluid in the
joints becomes solidified and interferes with our moving. On the other hand, too much liquidity interferes
with distension. North winds make for a certain proportion, so that we have strength and can stretch.

---

πνεύματος βαρεῖα ὑγρότης BON.    5. καὶ ὑγρότης βαρεῖα ἀντὶ
κούφου πνεύματος MAR.VAS. ὑγρότης βαρεῖα WI.   6-10. ἔτι δ'
ἡ μὲν ἰσχὺς καὶ δύναμις ἐν τοῖς ἀθρόοις τι. ἔπειτα μέντοι
κινεῖ λίαν δ' ὑγρὰ κεινένη συντίθεσθαι. τὰ δὲ βόρια ποιεῖ
τινα συμμετρίαν MSS.   7. ἄρθροις MAR.VAS. ἄρθροις ἐστί
SCHN. I   8. ἐπεὶ τὰ μέντοι κινεῖ λίαν δ' ὑγρὰ κωλύεται
συντείνεσθαι MAR.VAS.   9. βόρεια TURN. μόρια θέλει FURL.
70   7-10. ἐν τοῖς ἄρθροις ἐστί. ⟨ταῦτα δὲ ἀνίεται ὑπὸ τῶν
νοτίων·τὸ γὰρ γλίσχρον ἐν τοῖς ἄρθροις πεπηγὸς μὲν κωλύει⟩
κινεῖσθαι ἡμᾶς, ὑγρὸν δὲ λίαν ’ὸν συντείνεσθαι·τὰ δὲ βόρεια ποιεῖ τινα συμμετρίαν, ὥστε καὶ ἰσχύειν καὶ συντείνεσθαι BON.,SCHN. I   10. ἰσχὺν καὶ συντείνεσθαι μᾶλλον MSS.
ἴσχειν MAR.VAS. ἰσχύειν FURL. 70 μᾶλλον OM. FURL. 70

57.   καὶ πάλιν ξηροὶ καὶ μὴ ὑδατώδεις ὄντες ⟨οἱ⟩ νότοι
πυρετώδεις· ὑγρότητα γὰρ ἐνιᾶσι τοῖς σώμασι καὶ θέρμην
ἀλλοτρίαν [ἔσται] θερμοὶ φύσει καὶ ὑγροὶ ὄντες. ἡ δὲ τοιαύτη διάθεσις πυρετώδης· ὁ γὰρ πυρετὸς ⟨ἐξ⟩ ἀμφοῖν τούτοιν
ὑπερβολῆς ἐστιν. ὅταν ⟨δὲ⟩ ὑδάτινοι πνέωσι, τὸ ὕδωρ κατα-
ψύχει τὴν ἕξιν. τὸν αὐτὸν δὲ τρόπον καὶ ὅσα ἄλλα τῶν σωμάτων περὶ τὰς ἕξεις καθ᾽ ἑκάτερον συμβαίνει γίνεσθαι. πλείω
γάρ ἐστι τοιαῦτα καὶ ἐν πλείοσιν, ὧν ἁπάντων αἱ αὐταὶ καὶ
παραπλήσιαί τινες αἰτίαν.

58.   καὶ ⟨ἐπὶ⟩ τῶν καρπῶν δὲ καὶ τῶν ἄλλων τῶν τοιούτων
ὁμοίως· ἅπαντα γὰρ εἰς τὴν ὑγρότητα καὶ διάχυσιν καὶ τὴν
πυκνότητα καὶ σύστασιν καὶ ὅσα ἄλλα τῆς συστοιχίας ἑκατέρας
ἀναχθήσεται. καὶ ἐπὶ τῶν ἀψύχων δ᾽ ὡσαύτως, οἷον αἵ τε ῥηγ-
νύμεναι χορδαὶ καὶ οἱ ψόφοι τῶν κεκολλημένων καὶ ὅσα ἄλλα
συμβαίνει διυγραινομένων καὶ ἀνιεμένων, ⟨οἷον⟩ περὶ τὴν
τοῦ σιδήρου κατεργασίαν. πλείω γάρ φασιν ἐξελαύνειν τοῖς
νοτίοις ᾽ἢ βορείοις. αἴτιον δὲ ὅτι τὰ μὲν βόρεια ξηραίνει
καὶ σκληρύνει, τὰ δὲ νότια ἀνυγραίνει καὶ διαχεῖ· πᾶν δὲ
ἀργότερον διακεχυμένον ᾽ἢ ὑπεσκληρυμμένον·ἅμα δὲ καὶ μᾶλλον ἰσχύουσι καὶ συντονωτέρως ⟨ἔχουσι⟩ τοῖς βορείοις.

59.   ἁπλῶς δὲ τὰ μὲν τοιαῦτα χψεδὸν ἐμφανεῖς ἔχει τὰς
αἰτίας, οἷον ἀπὸ μιᾶς ἀρχῆς ἀνάλογον ἔχοντα τὸ ἐφεξῆς.

57.   1. παλίξηροι MSS. πάλιν ξηροὶ MAR.VAS. οἴοντες τόποι
MSS. ὄντες τόποι MAR.VAS.,BON. E VERS. TURN. ὄντες πυρετώ-
δεις FURL. 70 οἱ νότοι SCHN. V,LVII   2. γὰρ ἔνιοι MSS. γὰρ
ἐνίησι MAR.VAS. γὰρ ἐνιᾶσι SCHN. I θερμὴν ἄτε θερμοὶ MAR.
VAS. ⟨καὶ⟩ BON.   3. ἔσται θερμοὶ φύσει ἐμποιοῦσι θερμοὶ φύσει BON. ὑγρότητα γὰρ ἐν τοῖς σώμασι θερμὴν ἀλλοτρίαν ἐμποιοῦσι WI. τούτοις DOXZ ALD. τούτοιν CETT.   5.⟨δὲ⟩ MAR.VAS.
ὑδάτινα MSS. ὑδάτινοι SCHN. I   6. σωμάτων ἐστὶ τοιαῦτα
FURL. 106   7. περὶ ταῦτα ἐξῆς MSS. περὶ τὰς ἕξεις SCHN. I
ὥστε κατ᾽ ἑκάτερον FURL. 70

58.   1. ⟨ἐπὶ⟩ SCHN. II 598 δὴ MSS. δὲ SCHN. I   2. διά-

57. And again, south winds when dry and not rainy produce fever. Being normally warm and moist, they intro-
duce into the body an alien, warm moisture. This state
is conducive to fever, which is the result of an excess
of both qualities. But when the winds blow rainy, the
rain has a cooling effect on us. In the same way, whatever other physical conditions occur are due to each of
these qualities. There are many such effects in many
subjects, all of which have the same or similar causes.

58. It is thus also with crops and other such things.
For all bodies can be classified as to moisture, diffu-
sion, density, solidification, and any other aspects of
aggregation. Thus it is too with inanimate bodies such
as the breaking of gut strings and the cracking of glued
joints and the other things which occur when bodies are
moistened and slackened, as in the preparation oí iron.
For they say that iron can be beaten out better with
south winds than with north. The reason is that the
north winds dry and harden, while south winds moisten
and dissolve. A material is less resistant when soft-
ened than when it is hardened. But at the same time the
workers are stronger and more vigorous when the north
winds blow.

59. To sum up, such phenomena have fairly obvious

---

λυσιν MSS. διάχυσιν SCHN. I   6. ἀνιμένων CAM. ⟨οἷον⟩
SCHN. I E VERS. TURN.   8. νοτίοις EOM SCHN. I νοτείοις
CETT.,ALD.   9. διανθεῖ MSS. διανεῖ MAR.VAS. E VERS. TURN.
διαχεῖ FURL. 70 διαίνει SCHN. I   10. καὶ ὑπεσκληρυμένον
MSS. ’ἡ καὶ ὑπ. BON. ’ἠ ὑπ. SCHN. I ὑπεσκληρυμμένον SCHN.
V,LVII   11. ἴσχουσιν MSS. ἰσχύουσι SCHN. I συντονωτέρως
⟨ἔχουσιν⟩ τοῖς Βορείοις SCHN. V,LVII

59.   3. ἐν ἀπορίᾳ LPXZ MAR.VAS. ἡ ἀπορία CETT. ALD. τῆς
ἀπορίας καὶ ζητήσεως μᾶλλον δεῖται BON.   4. ⌊οἷον⌋ MAR.

ἐκεῖνο δ' ἐν ἀπορίᾳ καὶ ζητήσει μᾶλλον γίνεται καθ' ἑκάτερον ['ὀν], οἷον εἰ μὴ σκληρότης μηδὲ ξηρότης μηδὲ πυκνό-
της τοῖς βορείοις, ἀλλὰ τὰ ἐναντία. καὶ ⟨ἐπὶ⟩ τοῦ νότου δ'
ὡσαύτως. τὸ γὰρ παράλογον αἰτίαν ἐπιζητεῖ, τὸ δ' εὔλογον
καὶ ἄνευ αἰτίας συγχωροῦσιν οἱ ἄνθρωποι. δεινοὶ γὰρ προσ-
θεῖναι τὸ ἐλλιπές.

60.    ὅτι δὲ ψυχροὶ ὄντες οἱ ἄνεμοι ξηραίνουσι καὶ θᾶττον
⟨'ἢ⟩ ὁ ἥλιος θερμὸς 'ὢν, καὶ μάλιστα οἱ ψυχρότατοι ταύτην
ὑποληπτέον τὴν αἰτίαν, ὅτι ἀτμίδα ποιοῦσι, καὶ ταύτην ἀπά-
γουσι, καὶ οἱ ψυχρότεροι μᾶλλον· ὁ δὲ ἥλιος καταλείπει.διὰ
τί ποτε λέγεται· μή ποτ' ἀπ' ἠπείρου δείσης νέφος, ὡς ἀπὸ
πόντου χειμῶνος, θέρεος δὲ ἀπ' ἠπείροιο μελαίνης; ἢ διότι τοῦ μὲν χειμῶνος ἡ θάλαττα θερμοτέρα, ὥστε εἴ τι ⟨συν-
έστη,δῆλον ὅτι ἀπ' ἀρχῆς⟩ συνέστηκεν ἰσχυρᾶς. ἐλύθη γὰρ
'ἂν τῷ ἀέρι, διὰ τὸ ἀλεεινὸν εἶναι τὸν τόπον. τοῦ δὲ θέρους ἡ μὲν θάλαττα ψυχρὰ καὶ τὰ πόντια πνεύματα, ἡ δὲ γῆ
θερμή·ὥστε εἴ τι ἀπὸ τῆς γῆς ⟨φέρεται, διὰ μείζονος ἀρχῆς⟩
συνέστη· διελύθη γὰρ 'ἂν, εἰ ἀσθενὴς ἦν.

61.    τὸ δὲ μὴ πνεῖν νότον λαμπρὸν ἐν Αἰγύπτῳ  μηδ' ἡμέρας
δρόμον ἀπέχοντι καὶ νυκτὸς,ψεῦδος.δασύνειν δὲ τὸν οὐρανὸν

---

VAS.,FORT. BON.    5. ⟨ἐπὶ⟩ MAR.VAS.    6. ἐπιζητεῖν MSS.
ἐπιζητεῖ MAR.VAS.    7. συγχωροῦσι...ἐλλιπὲς OM. FURL. 107
⟨ἄνθρωποι⟩ καὶ γὰρ αὐτοὶ δεινοὶ SCHN. I δεινοὶ γὰρ προσ-
θεῖναι WI.

60. 2. ⟨'ἢ⟩ FURL. 71 ψυχρότατοι ⟨ὄντες ἄνεμοι⟩ MAR.VAS.
DEL. SCHN. II 599,WI.    4. κατα LAC. 9 LITT. DLMQUXZ ALD.
καταδεῖν EIOR καταλείπει P₁ FURL. 71 καταλήπει P₂ διὰ τί
δὲ BON.    5. μὴ [ποτ'] FURL. 71 ἀπ' ἠπείρου MSS. ἠπείροιο
EGO    6. θέρος DLOXZ ALD. θέρεος IMPQRU θέρους BON.    7.
ὡς ἐπὶ IQRXZ ὡς ἐπεὶ CETT. ALD. ὥστε εἴ τι MAR.VAS. ὥστε
εἴ τις FURL. 71. ⟨συνέστη,δῆλον ὅτι ἀπ' ἀρχῆς FURL. 71  9.
τοῦτο θέρους IXZ τοῦτε θέρους CETT. ALD. τοῦ δὲ θέρους

causes, as for example, having a logical consequence derived from a single original principle. But the following is more problematical for both winds, namely, if the
north winds do not make for hardness nor dryness nor density, but rather the opposite, and so too with the south
winds. It is the anomalous which calls for explanation;
we accept the reasonable without inquiry into causation
and are intelligent enough to fill the gap.

60. The reason that winds which are cold dry more quickly than the sun, which is warm, and the coldest winds
most of all, must be that they create a vapor and remove
it, especially the coldest winds, while the sun leaves
the vapor. And why do people say, "Do not fear a cloud
from the land in winter as much as one from the sea, but
do fear one in the summer from the dark land."? Is it
because the sea is the warmer in the winter, so that if
some cloud forms, it obviously arises from a strong
source? Otherwise it would have been dissipated in the
air because the region is warm. In summer the sea is
cool and so are the sea breezes, while the land is warm.
**Thus, if a cloud moves off the land, it has been formed**
from a stronger source. If the source had been weak,
the cloud would have dispersed.

61. The belief that the south wind does not blow strong
in Egypt for a day and a night's journey (from the coast)

---

SCHN. I  11. τῆς γῆς MSS. OM.SCHN. I,REST. II 599 ⟨φέρε-
ται, διὰ μείζονος ἀρχῆς⟩ SCHN. I   12. εἰς ἀσθένειαν MSS.
εἰ ἀσθενὴς ἦν MAR.VAS. εἰ ἀσθενὲς ἦν SCHN. I

61.  1. νότου λαμπροῦ MSS. νότον λαμπρὸν TURN.,MAR.VAS.
2. ἀπέχοντα BON. 3. αἴθριον φέρειν SC. φασὶ FURL. 107 αἱ

μάλιστα βορέαν καὶ ἀργέστην, τὸν δὲ νότον παραφέρειν. τοὺς
δὲ ἔωθεν ἐπινεφεῖν καὶ δασύνειν, ἄχρις 'ἂν ὁ ἥλιος ἀνίσχῃ·
οὐχ ὕειν δὲ διὰ τὸ μὴ ἔχειν ὅπου προσκαθίζηται τὰ νέφη. νότον δὲ καὶ εὖρον καὶ ὅσα ἀπὸ μεσημβρίας, ἄρχεσθαι μὲν ἀπὸ
ἀνατολῶν, συμπαραχωρεῖν δὲ τῷ ἡλίῳ· βορέαν δὲ καὶ ἀργέστην
ἀνάπαλιν ἀπὸ δυσμῶν ἐπ' ἀνατολάς.

62. ἐν Σικελίᾳ ⟨δὲ⟩ καικίαν οὐ καλοῦσιν ἀλλ' ἀπηλιώτην·
δοκεῖ δ' οὐχ ὁ αὐτὸς εἶναί τισιν, ἀλλὰ διαφέρειν. ὅτι ὁ
μὲν δασύνει τὸν οὐρανὸν, ὁ δ' οὔ. ...ἀργέστην δὲ...οἱ μὲν
[οὖν] ὀλυμπίαν, οἱ δὲ σκίρωνα καλοῦσιν, οἱ ⟨δὲ⟩ περὶ Σικελίαν κιρκίαν. τὸν ἀπηλιώτην ⟨δὲ⟩ ἑλλησποντίαν, κάρβαν δὲ
Φοίνικες, βερεκ⟨υντίαν⟩ δ' ⟨οἱ⟩ ἐν τῷ Πόντῳ.

---

δ' ἔωθεν MSS. ἔτι δὲ ἔωθεν MAR.VAS. αἱ δὲ αὖραι ἔωθεν MAR.
VAS.₂ τὸ δ' ἔωθεν BON. τοὺς δὲ ἔωθεν FURL. 71    4. ἐπινή-
φειν MSS. ἐπινίφειν BON. ἐπινέφειν FURL. 71 ἐπινεφεῖν
SCHN. I ἀνίσχῃ DLMXZ ALD. ἀνίσχειν CETT. ἀνίσχῃ SCHN. I
5. προκαθήσεται EOUZ₁ προκαθίσηται Z₂CETT. ALD. προσκαθίζηται SCHN. I

62.   1. ⟨δὲ⟩ καικίαν MAR.VAS.,SCHN. I καικίαν δ' οὐ MSS.
οὐ OM. MAR.VAS.,HEINS. καταπορθμίαν BON.    3. ὁ δ' οὐ LAC.
16 LITT. πάρεγγυς δὲ LAC. 18 LITT. οἱ μὲν οὖν ὀλυμπίαν
MSS. ἀργέστην δὲ οἱ μὲν [οὖν] ὀλυμπίαν BON.    4. καλοῦσιν
ὑπὲρ σικελίαν MSS. καλοῦσιν οἱ περὶ Σικελίαν FURL. 71
καλοῦσιν οἱ ⟨δὲ⟩ περὶ Σικελίαν SCHN. I    5. δερκίαν MSS.
κίρκιαν MAR.VAS. ἰάπυγα BON. κερκίαν SALMASIUS 1258 κιρκίαν BOEKER 2306-7 ⟨δὲ⟩ SCHN. I    6. βερει LAC. 7-14 LITT.
MSS. βερέκιν MAR.VAS. βερεκυντίαν FURL. 71,SCHN. I    δ'
⟨οἱ⟩ SCHN. I

is false. They say that the north wind and the west-
north-west wind cloud tne sky most, while the south wind
blows the clouds aside. Winds at dawn bring clouds and
darken the sky until the sun rises. Because the clouds
have no place to settle, there is no rain. The south
wind, the south-east wind, and all other winds from the
south start from sunrise and follow the sun. The north
wind and the west-north-west wind on the contrary proceed from sundown to sunrise.

62. In Sicily they call the wind not Caecias (east-
north-east) but Apeliotes (east). Some think it is not
the same wind because the one darkens the sky, the other
does not. Some call Argestes (west-north-west) Olympias,
others call it Skiron; in Sicily it is called Circias.
Apeliotes is called Hellespontias, the Phoenicians call
it Carbas, the people in the region of Pontus call it
Berecyntias.

# COMMENTARY

(Figures within sections refer to the lines
of the Greek text)

Section 1.  References: <u>Meteorologica</u> I 13, 349a 19-32;
II 4, 5, 6.

4.  Theophrastus is in agreement with Aristotle in opposing the sea-of-air doctrine.  Cf. Böker 2227.

9.  That part of the sky occupied by air, the sublunary,
Bonaventura.

Section 2.  Reff.: <u>Meteor.</u>  361a 5-15; 364a 27-30; <u>Prob-</u>
<u>lemata</u> 26, 15; 26, 35; Böker 2332; 2240-1; Gilbert, p.
528.

7.  The history of the two-wind theory is discussed by
Böker, 2332.  There can be little doubt of the accuracy
of this observation, as all modern data from Greece support the dominance in force and frequency of the north
and south winds.  The Theophrastean explanation is innovative in that a mechanical exchange is envisioned, following the direct action of the sun, without the neces-
sity of the auxiliary mechanism, the dry exhalation.  In
a very rough way, Theophrastus is close to the correct
explanation, as the mean seasonal atmospheric pressure
patterns over the Balkans and eastern Mediterranean
responsible for north and south winds are a response in
turn to the annual apparent course of the sun and to the
geography of the area.

Reitzenstein, p. 103 (47): The air condenses in the east, the west, the north, and the south.

Section 3.  Reff.: Meteor.  358a 29ss; Prob. 23, 16; 26, 48; 26, 52; 26, 16; 26, 49.

5.  This concept reappears in Sections 19 and 20.  Böker 2231 comments on the false theory of the ancients that air subjected to compression becomes cold, while that which expands becomes hot.  This impression arose through the physiological cooling which occurred as the breath was blown through the mouth on the fingers, and it prevented the ancients from recognizing thermal differences as causes for winds.

6.  What may have given rise to this notion is the fact that in winter the northern African desert is cool and supplies relatively cool air to the warm sectors of depressions.  Compressional heating along the Libyan coast and travel across the warmer Mediterranean may make them appear as warmer winds by the time they arrive in Greece.

Section 4.  Reff.: Meteor.  361b 5-10; Prob. 26, 56; Gilbert, p. 579.

5.  The analogy to hydrology is developed here.

6.  Gilbert, p. 579, comments on the reciprocity implied here.  The moisture acquired by the south wind in its passage across the Mediterranean foretells rain for those

in the more northerly areas; the idea that the etesians
were rainy south and east of Greece may be derived from
the fact that as the etesians progress southwards across
the Mediterranean, cumulus clouds form and showers may
occur along elevated coastlines (Great Britain, Meteorological Office, Weather in the Mediterranean, 2nd Edition, Vol. 1, 1964, London, p. 78). Showers may occur
also in the south Balkans and occasionally as far south
as Athens at the onset of an etesian period. (Metaxas,
Howell and Karapiperis, Interpretation of the Rainfall
Climate of Marathon, Greece, Athens, 1952, p. 114).

Section 5. Reff.: Meteor. 361b 2-5; Prob. 26, 7; 26,
19; 26, 20; 26, 27; 26, 39; 26, 41; 26, 45; 26, 52;
26, 56; De Signis 29.
6. From Prob. 26, 20 and 26, 45 the full saying: "Sail
when the south wind commences and the north wind is
dying down." The proverb probably derived from the
sequence of winds accompanying cyclonic passage through
eastern Europe. The southerly winds in front of the
cyclone gradually increase in velocity, the northerly
winds behind the cold front to the rear of the cyclone
decrease in velocity.
8. Like rivers, winds pick up tributaries.

Section 6. Reff.: Prob. 25, 18; 26, 20; 26, 38; 26, 62.
1. The statement is not correct. Northerly winds dom-

inate in Egypt and Libya, except near the immediate coast. Theophrastus appears to be fitting facts to theories.

7. "Places proper to it," Egypt and Libya. Air currents flowing southward in the northern hemisphere tend to diverge with decreasing cloudiness, while those moving northward tend to converge with increasing cloudiness, thus providing a meteorological basis for the statement.

Section 7. Reff.: <u>Prob.</u> 26, 19; 26, 20; 26, 38; 26, 45; 26, 62; <u>De Signis</u> 35.

2. The clouds freeze and become heavier; they are unable to be driven by the winds, thus only the force, but not the coldness is transferred.

8. The south wind collects more air as it blows along, air which does not freeze, being collected from a warm area. Consequently it accumulates, condenses, and so brings rainfall.

9. "Source" means both amount of matter and force (Bonaventura).

Section 8. Reff.: <u>Prob.</u> 26, 44 and Section 61.

1. In fact, the wind data suggest just the opposite. Southerly winds are more frequent, particularly in winter, at Alexandria, on the coast. In Upper Egypt, northerly winds dominate throughout the year. Northerly winds are constant enough upstream from Cairo so that boats can

journey upstream under sail and float downstream. (W. Kendrew, Climates of the Continents, 3d edition, New York, 1942, p. 49).

Section 9. Reff.: Prob. 26, 46; 26, 47; Böker 2241.
1. Böker 2241 for the historical background of this concept. In antiquity shelter was sought on the south sides of islands, as a sudden swing of the wind toward the south was uncommon. On the other hand, anchoring along the north sides of islands was advised against, as sudden north winds could cast the ships against a rocky coast. This belief probably resulted from the suddenness with which boras and squalls from the north occurred along the Greek coast.

Section 10. Reff.: Section 2; Meteor. 361a 5-23; Prob. 26, 2; 26, 3; 26, 16; Strohm (B), pp. 256ss; Section 33; Pliny, Nat. Hist. II 47; De Signis 7.
3. The statement is remarkably accurate and could result only from carefully kept wind data.
6-11. Reitzenstein, p. 103 (48): Air condenses and is drawn by the void, which draws vapor from the water and from the earth and thus becomes filled.
11. The Pleiades set in the morning ca. November 9 and set in the evening ca. March 27.

Section 11. Reff.: Meteor. 362a 11-20; Prob. 26, 2; 26, 10; 26, 51; Böker 2213s; 2247; 2258s; 2310s.

3. The white south winds, leuconoti, arise at a definite time after the winter solstice and are winds of fair weather.

4. ἀσυννεφεῖς, because γὰρ applies to both adjectives to explain "white" south winds.

6. Wimmer glosses "Such is the nature of the etesians," since there is no discussion other than the one special point. Steinmetz, p. 31, suggests a lacuna here.

7. We retain the negative with Section 12, 1, Prob. 26, 51, and Meteor. 362a 2.

11. The ancients differed as to when the precursors blew. Modern data indicate they begin in early May.

Section 12. Reff.: Meteor. 362a 17-31; 366a 17; Prob. 25, 2; 25, 16; 26, 51.

1. The etesians are the subject of the sentence. The diurnal variability is one of the most marked features of the etesians.

4-6. It appears that the material of the winds here is moisture, contrary to Meteor. 360a 12-13.

6-7. Steinmetz, p. 32, believes these lines refer to the motion of the sun annually. The year-to-year strength and intensity of the etesians vary in correlation with sun-spot activity. (Carapiperis, On the Periodicity of Etesians at Athens, p. 379). There is no indication of annual variation here, however.

Section 13.

1. A general cooling, beginning about 500 B.C., accompanied the Sub-Atlantic stage in Europe. (Lamb, The Changing Climate, p. 6).

10. Theophrastus, like Aristotle, believed the etesians occurred as a result of melting snow, Section 11; hence they must have been more forceful in his time than earlier.

Section 14.

1. On Aristaeus and the winds, Apollonius Rhodius II 500ss; Pauly-Wissowa II 1 854. Ceos is not far from Cape Sunium. Theophrastus reasons that with less snow in the milder period of the past and therefore with less material for the etesians, they were less forceful.

8. Steinmetz, p. 34, believes that the lacuna in the mss. once contained a statement of long-term weather changes (Cf. Regenbogen 1410). The last sentence in the section seems to argue against this.

8-9. For the influence of wind on plants, Section 43 and De Causis Plantarum III 3, 3. Steinmetz, p. 34, cites the transition from a grain diet to a meat diet (from Theophrastus' De Pietate) as confirmation of the long-term weather trend.

Section 15. Reff.: Meteor. 360a 3s; 361b 14-23; Prob. 25, 4; 25, 7; 26, 34; Gilbert pp. 531s.

2. The sun can impart motion, but the exhalation has a
motion of its own (Bonaventura). The exhalation seems to
be both material cause and cooperating efficient cause.
But the sun is the primary cause.

4. Reitzenstein, p. 102 (44): Winds originate from
above or below, those from below derive from earth or
water. The wind moves upward because of its lightness.

7. Here Theophrastus is talking about the moist exhalation, not the dry, as having effect.

Section 16.

3. The proportion is that of the action of the sun and
the amount of moisture raised, as in Section 15; Steinmetz, p. 37.

5. The drying up of the wind supports the conception of
wind as moisture.

Section 17. Reff.: <u>Meteor.</u> 361b 14-17; <u>De Generatione
Animalium</u> 738a 20; 777b 24; <u>De Signis</u> 5; Böker 2263.

1. Meteorologists, after long discarding extraterres-
trial influences, have discovered statistical evidence
of lunar influences, particularly as to precipitation.
The physical link is the atmospheric tides. (Glenn W.
Brier, "Diurnal and Semidiurnal Tides in Relation to Precipitation Variations," <u>Monthly Weather Review</u>, Vol. 93,
No. 2, Feb., 1965, pp. 93-100).

6. Wood-Symons translate κατὰ σύμπτωμα "according to a

regular occurrence",though Liddell and Scott does not
give this meaning. Since the usual meaning "by chance"
could not conform to an attempt to ascertain cause-and-
effect relationships, we have chosen "in conjunction" in
partial agreement with the thought of Wood-Symons.

Section 18. Reff.: Meteor. 366a 15-18; Prob. 25, 4; 25,
7; De Signis 33; Böker 2245 and 2260.
1. "The same cause" refers to what follows, the sun as
cause of wind and disturbance.
3. "This sort of air" refers to the moist exhalation.
The belief as to these daily variations probably arose
from the diurnal characteristics of the bora, a cold,
dry wind from the north or northwest, which blows sometimes in violent gusts down from the mountains on the
eastern shore of the Adriatic, and which exhibited a
principal minimum about midnight, and the characteristics of the etesians at Athens, which reached their maximum velocity before noon, and then decreased in velocity as a result of sea breeze. Cf. also Böker 2245 and
2260, in which the bora is also held responsible for the
belief in midnight and midday stoppages or calms.

Section 19. Reff.: Prob. 25, 19; 26, 48.
2. In Meteor. 341a 13-32 the sun causes heat by its
motion through friction, not by being hot itself, as here
in Theophrastus.

5. Bonaventura's ἐμπίπτουσα seems supported by Prob.
25, 48.

7-8. Strohm (B), p. 253, considers this a new idea. The
temperature of the wind is determined by the place of
exit (origin) and the nature of the air during the trav-
erse.

Section 20. Reff.: Meteor. 367a 34-b4; Prob. 25, 10;
26, 48; 34, 7; Strohm (A), p. 50; Strohm (B), pp. 252-3.
4. Steinmetz, p. 40, believes the narrows through which
the first material passes are the spaces between the air
particles, the material being the rays of the sun. But
the comparison with the mouth suggests merely gross phenomena, not atomistic channels.

Section 21.
Steinmetz, p. 41, suggests that heat stored in the earth
after the sun has delivered it there is contributive to
making the local air torrid.

Section 22. Reff.: Meteor. 342a 24-27; 361a 22-25;
Prob. 25, 14; 26, 36; 26, 48.
3-6. Wood-Symons criticize the reasoning here. There
should be no motion, only equilibrium. The thought is
taken almost verbatim from Meteor. 342a 24-27. Signifi-
cantly, Theophrastus does not appeal to the apparent
circular motion of the heavens. For him the condition
of the air, where heat and cold cancel out vertical

motion and leave open the possibility of horizontal motion, is more important than the motion of the celestial sphere.

5. Schneider, V, 160 points out that both breath and vapor tend to rise.

Section 23. Reff.: Prob. 23, 16; 26, 30.

1. The moist exhalation, Steinmetz, p. 43.

3. Steinmetz, p. 44, suggests adding καὶ τῇ θερμότητι since Section 25 in this group deals with hot winds.

Section 24.

4. αὖραι are local breezes, Steinmetz, p. 44. They originate from the movement of moisture, Flashar, p. 654.

Section 25. Ref.: Prob. 26, 16.

1. For the breezeless Nile, Herodotus 2, 27.

Section 26. Reff.: Section 53; Prob. 25, 22; 26, 4; 26, 5; 26, 40.

1. Reversing winds (sea breezes) provide the keynote for the mechanical interplay of the winds. They are analogous to the flux and reflux in narrow channels.

5. The sea is viewed as a hollow collecting-place for wind.

8. Land breezes are weak because of the comparatively slight moist exhalation on land, Steinmetz, p. 45.

Section 27. Ref.: Böker 2257.

3-7. Ossa and Olympus in Thessaly; Aegae, now Edhessa,
lies at the foot of the vegetation-bare south wall of
the Bora Massif, and east of Begorittis Lake. A combination lake-and-valley breeze occurs in opposition to the
prevailing northerly flow. A similar phenomenon occurs
near Athens, where the sea breeze is in opposition to the
etesians. The countercurrent is reached at an elevation
of about 1000 meters (An der Lan, p. 12).

Section 28. Ref.: Böker 2258.

3-6. The counterwinds of the Palimboreas occur as the
etesians are blocked by the mountains of Euboea and
strong surface heating on the west-and-south-facing
slopes cause indrafts of air in opposition to the prevailing etesians. These breezes have been confirmed at
300 to 700 meters above the surface by fliers (An der
Lan, p. 5).

Section 29. Reff.: Meteor. 370b 18ss; 363a 1ss; Prob.
26, 2; 26, 48; Böker 2230ss; 2254.

2. The theory of increase in wind force through narrows
was extended to an explanation of the force of the etesians, to north winds in general, and to various fallwinds along the south slopes of mountains.

7. Theophrastus is in flat contradiction to Aristotle,
who denies, Meteor. 349a 16-32 and 361a 30-32, that wind

is air in motion.

Section 30. Ref.: Hippocrates, De Sanorum Victu 2, 1.
5. The reduced friction over water surfaces leads to
higher wind velocities over islands and lee shore areas.
8. The concept of a wind running out of energy seems to
be opposed to the concept of the stream gathering in from
tributaries as it proceeds, Section 7.

Section 31.
5. Cf. Carapiperis, The Etesian Winds, Part VI, "On the
Daily Variation of the Velocity of the Etesian Winds in
Athens." Etesian winds reach their maximum velocities in
the afternoon over the open sea. On lands where sea
breezes occur, the reversing winds develop at about the
time when the etesians over the open sea are becoming
strongest. Thus "the reversing wind blows against the
land winds, and the etesians rise at the same time
again." This follows the noon lull, when the sea breeze
is being established.

Section 32.
3. Plataea is at an elevation of about 500 meters on the
north slope of Mt. Cithaeron (1400 meters). Mountains to
the north may block off the north winds. Plataea may be
subjected to fallwinds when the scirocco blows, which may
become very strong on the leeward (north) slopes of Mt.
Cithaeron. Section 45 gives a clear layman's descrip-

tion of the fallwind.

7. Carystus in Euboea is located at the extreme south-east tip, protected by mountains (Ikji Oros, 1398 meters) to the north and east. The location is such that strong sea breezes in conjunction with valley breezes occur. Heating of the south-facing slopes in combination with the contrast in temperature between the land and sea would account for a reversal of the etesians in that area.

Section 33.
Phaestus is on the southernmost promontory of Cyprus called today Akrotiri. The wave, generated by wind far out to sea, has its power enhanced by the configuration of the shoreline. Theophrastus believed that the promontory was protected by a buffer of air and consequently the wind responsible for the wave was prevented from reaching the shore. The analogy is made to a breeze through the windows of a house with the door closed.

Section 34. Ref.: Böker 2305.
2-3. Reitzenstein, p. 103 (50): Winds arise from above when water aloft dissolves or when many exhalations arise. The stormwind is caused when winds collide with clouds or with the air circulating aloft so that there is a reversal toward the earth. Stormwinds descend from above; winds blow from the water and from mountains.

4. The kataigis (fallwind) was interpreted by Aristotle
as within the theory of lightning and outside the framework of wind theory. Theophrastus correctly places the
kataigis within wind theory without utilization of the
dry exhalation. Cf. H. Strohm, "Theophrast und Pose-
idonios," Hermes 81, p. 283.

Section 35. Reff.: Meteor. 361a 28s; Prob. 23, 2; 23,
11; 23, 12; 23, 28; Böker 2237.

Section 36. Reff.: Prob. 26, 23; 26, 25; De Signis 13
and 37.
6. In Prob. 26, 25 read λοιπὸν rather than θερμὸν,
Flashar, p. 683.

Section 37. Reff.: Meteor. 361b 4-14; Prob. 26, 1; 26,
29; De Signis 36; Böker 2252.
5. Salmasius, p. 1259 suggests κα'ι'κίας after the
river Kaikus in Mysia. The verse would then read: ἕλκων
ἐφ' αὐτὸν ὡς κα'ι'κίας νέφη, an iambic hexameter, Böker
2252. Cold air masses from the Crimea-Caucasus area rush
through the Bosporus-Dardanelles into the North Aegean
toward Greece, pushing low-lying cloud banks ahead of
them. The phenomenon is relatively common (An der Lan, p.
395). Hence the proverb "drawing clouds to himself like
the east-north-east wind." The situation is not unlike
occurrences in the Great Lakes area of North America,
where cold northwesterly winds passing over warmer lake

waters result in squally and cloudy weather.

Section 38.  Reff.: Prob. 26, 31; 26, 33; 26, 36; 26, 52.
2.  Data support the statement that west winds are most
frequent in spring and late autumn.
3.  For the west wind in Homer: Iliad 23, 200; Odyssey 5,
295; 5, 332; 12, 289; 14, 458 and perhaps 4, 567.
4.  Philoxenus: not otherwise known.

Section 39.  Reff.: Meteor. 364b 12-14; Prob. 26, 1; 26,
29; De Signis 3; Böker 2251-2.
2.  Caecias, the east-north-east wind, was accompanied
by squall clouds or roller clouds supported by very
strong indrafts.  Its marked cloud-forming characteristics induced the ancients to explain it as a wind which
moved circularly, with the hollow part of its path of
travel toward the sky.  Thus blowing toward its beginning, it conveys clouds to itself.  But Prob. 26, 1 has
it blowing from above with its curvature toward the
earth.

Section 40.  Reff.: Prob. 25, 10; 26, 31; 26, 52.
7.  Most mss. of Prob. 26, 52 give ὕλην  or ἵλην
Flashar, p. 691 prefers the former, but Meteor. 364a 25ss
support εἵλην  from the latter reading; west winds are
exposed to the sun less time than the east winds.
7.  This wind can go into motion by itself.  This is a
departure from Aristotelian doctrine, which cannot

explain the motion of saturated breezes. The west wind, blowing off vaporizing water, moves under its own power, not subjected to the strict control of the sun.

Section 41. Reff.: Prob. 26, 31; 26, 35; 26, 52; Böker 2230s.

3. Böker believes that this section makes it clear that there was a doctrine according to which south winds had their origin by analogy to north winds, that is, flowing through narrow constrictions in E-W mountain ranges. The west wind, however, is a level wind and "flows gently as through a pipe."

5. Data confirm the afternoon periodicity of the west wind alluded to here.

Section 42. Ref.: Prob. 26, 24.

Section 43. Reff.: Prob. 26, 17; 26, 31; 26, 52.

Section 44.

4. For Locris, Strabo VI 1, 7-8. Böker 2249 states that Locri in Bruttium does not answer the description. Perhaps Krisa in Locris on the Krisaean Gulf, now Gulf of Salona near Corinth, was meant. But the mss. are clear on Italy.

7. The land slopes westward from Gortyna toward the Libyan Sea, a broad valley opening to the west; hence the observation seems correct (Pauly-Wissowa VII 2, 1667

s. v. Gortyn).

Section 45.  Ref.: Böker 2258.

1.  Both the Malic Gulf and the Pierian region near Thessaly are subjected to strong downslope winds when the west wind is blowing.

2.  The mss. read "kierion," which is near Pharsalus in Thessaly, but Pieria, north of Thessaly on the Thermaic Gulf, to the west of which is Mt. Pierus, is open to the east to a greater extent than Kierion.

5-10.  If Meteor.  340b 36-341a 2 is genuine--Strohm (A), pp. 66-67 denies its authenticity--, Theophrastus is in flat contradiction of Aristotle, who cited plausible evidence to show that there is no wind on mountain tops. Prob. 26, 36 also speaks of air moving on mountain tops.

Section 46.

4.  The original text of this proverb is lost.

6.  The proverb is given as two hexameter lines in Prob. 26, 46.

7.  The reasoning is inverted here.  Theophrastus assumes that the moisture over rivers, in the form of mists and fogs, has resulted in cooling of the air, instead of the cooling of the air resulting in the manifestation of the moisture.

Section 47.  Reff.: Prob. 26, 21; 26, 35; 26, 54; Böker 2256; 2261-2; Meteor.  364b 14.

In this section the mechanical interchange of air which occurs on a seasonal basis is extended to diurnal behavior. Data do not offer any factual support for this.

Section 48. Reff.: <u>Meteor</u>. 361b 30-35; <u>Prob</u>. 26, 12; 26, 32; Böker 2256; ?262.

8. Sirius rises in the morning July 15.

8. Wood-Symons interpret τὰ κάτω as the lower part of the atmosphere; Bonaventura and Flashar, p. 681 as "south of Greece." We follow the latter two. The sun is nearly overhead in the southern areas (Tropic of Cancer). Southerly winds would occur, except for the interference of the etesians caused by the melting of the far northern snow (Theophrastus).

Section 49. Reff.: <u>Prob</u>. 26, 9; 26, 11; 26, 14.

1-6. Flashar, pp. 218 and 680 interprets the passage in <u>Prob</u>. 26, 9 to mean that the three-day term comes under the Pythagorean rule of three explicated in <u>De Caelo</u> 268a 6-14. Thus he thinks that all winds are limited to three days. But the succeeding passage about the south winds in this section rules that out. Wood-Symons believe, correctly, that the weakest north winds end before the three-day term has run out, but take πρώτη to mean "early on the third day." We are inclined to take the adjective partitively but to derive from the "weakest" the shortest possible term. Hence "on the first day of the triad."

2. The proverb in dactylic hexameter in Greek.

3. North winds are caused by melting snows, according
to Theophrastus. Melting ceases or goes on slowly at
night; thus an incipient nocturnal north wind is weak.

Section 50. Reff.: Meteor. 365a 2-6; Prob. 26, 3; 26,
14; De Signis 34, 36, 37; Böker 2253; 2295.

2-3. Wood-Symons identify the run-on line as a possible
iambic verse: ἀπ᾽ ἀσθενοῦς γὰρ οὐδέν ἐστ᾽ ἀρχῆς μέγα,
Reitzenstein, p. 102 (45): "We see that the stormwinds
descend from the clouds and we see the winds blow from
the water and from the mountains."

4.   φιλεῖ....πάχνην part of a dactylic hexameter, Steinmetz, p. 50.

5. Concoction and purification refer to weather events
accompanying the passage of squall lines. Cf. Meteor.
360b 25-30; 381a 24; Böker 2234. The ancients referred
to the strong indrafts associated with a squall line as
"cooking" or "boiling up" of the air. After the rain or
hail occurs, the winds usually drop. This, to the
ancients, was a sign of purification. The concoction is
the warm air indraft to the squall, which is "cooked" and
purified by release of moisture.

Section 51.

3. Lips, the west-south-west wind is described as wet

and cloud-forming; Argestes, the west-north-west wind is dry, bringing fair weather, <u>Meteor</u>. 364b 24-25. 4-5. The proverb is an elegiac distich, Steinmetz, p. 50.

Section 52. Reff.: <u>Meteor</u>. 364b 14-18; <u>Prob</u>. 26, 12; 26, 26, 31; 26, 55; Böker 2262; Flashar, pp. 685-6. Böker mentions a clockwise succession of the winds. This succession would be observed with the approach of a cyclone and its subsequent path north of Greece. In <u>Prob</u>. 26, 26 the veering is said to follow the course of the sun; in <u>Prob</u>. 26, 31 and 26, 55 the direction of the shift is clockwise; in 26, 12 the shift is not clearly defined. Flashar, p. 685: "The winds turn either to their opposites or to the right"; the doctrine of the turning of the winds (<u>Meteor</u>. 364b 14; <u>De Ventis</u> 52) is contradictory in the <u>Problems</u> as well as with respect to Aristotle and Theophrastus. There can be no doubt that "turning of the winds to the right" is seen here from the north, if the west lies to the right of the north and the western Zephyrus blows after the northern Boreas. The same circular movement is to be found in the Corpus Hippocraticum, <u>De Hebdomadis</u> 3. In contradiction to this it is stated in <u>Prob</u>. 26, 55 that the eastern Apeliotes swings around into the southern Notus, Notus into Zephyrus, and Zephyrus in turn into Boreas. Here then the circular swing is seen in reverse. This direction seems

more natural when we consider that according to Aristotle
and Theophrastus the turning of the winds goes by the
path of the sun (Meteor. 364b 14ss), but seems to be
conceived clockwise. Gilbert, p. 581 remarks on the
turning of the winds that the observations agree in the
ascertaining of these facts; in detail, however, the
results of the observations part company.

Section 53. Reff.: Meteor. 344b 35-37; Prob. 26, 5; 26,
40.

5. The Idyris River is on the west side of the Pamphylian Gulf on the south coast of Turkey. The gulf lacks
offshore islands. The land to the west is mountainous
and the area is very likely to be subjected to fallwinds.

7. Meteor. 364a 27-29, however, states that winds dia-
metrically opposite to each other do not blow against
each other.

8. Meteor. 371a 15-18: a "prester" is whirlwind with
much fire. For Theophrastus, water, converted to vapor
and mist, is the matter of the winds. That is why the
"prester" is not a firewind, Steinmetz, p. 173.
Reitzenstein, p. 103 (49): When one puts the open end of
a pipe to the surface of water and sucks out the air, we
have something comparable to the stormwind which arises
from below.

Section 55. Reff.: Meteor. 361b 30-35; Prob. 26, 13.

2. Orion rises in early July and sets in Mid-November.
5-7. The instability of the winds during the atmospheric
transition periods was readily detected by the Greeks.
Data indicate that winds at Athens in November are direc-
tionally unstable.

Section 56. Reff.: Prob. 1, 24; 26, 42; Hippocrates,
De Morbo Sacro 13.
3. The increase in warmth and humidity brought about by
the south wind in the Aegean is a common event. These
humid sciroccos are called "Garbi" winds in the Aegean
(E. R. Biel, Climatology of the Mediterranean Area, 1944,
p. 18.).

Section 57. Reff.: Prob. 1, 23; 26, 50.

Section 58. Reff.: Prob. 1, 24; De Signis 30.

Section 60. Reff.: Prob. 25, 18; 26, 28; 26, 57.
1-4. It is colder when the north wind blows; the south
wind attracts clouds, while the north wind repels them;
there is more evaporation with a north wind and more in
winter than in summer, Prob. 25, 18.
4-5. The proverb is in hexameters in the Greek text.
Cf. Prob. 25, 7. The proverb alludes to the differential seasonal capacities of land vis-à-vis water bodies
in inducing convective cloud development.

Section 61. Reff.: Sections 5 and 8; Prob. 26, 44.

Section 62. Reff.: Pseudo-Aristotle, De Situ et Nomini-
bus Ventorum.

1. "Caecias...a local name for the northwest (30 degrees
from 0 to north) wind, which blew down the Caicus valley
from Pergamum to Titane and entered the circle of general
winds," Böker 2305.

3. "Argestes" as an adjective, "bright, clear," could
apply to several winds. Hesiod, Theogony 379, uses it
for Zephyrus. Olympias was known in Euboea, Hist. Plant.
IV 14, 11; Causae Plant. V 12, 4, coming from Pierian
Olympus; the Lesbian Olympias was probably not a northwest wind, Böker 2309-2310. Sciron, blowing from the
Megarid into the Saronic Gulf, would come at sailors making for Piraeus as a west-north-west wind, Böker 2320.
Circias blows from Mt. Circeius on the Latin coast, but
the name generalized to northwest winds along the entire
Tyrrhenian coast from Marseille to Sicily, Böker 2306-7.
Hellespontias blows with especial vigor for several weeks
in the summer through the Bosporus and the Dardanelles,
with their narrow bed and high banks, toward Cape Sigeum,
Böker 2298-99.

5. Carbas is perhaps identifiable with a wind blowing
from Carpasia in Cyprus. It was an east wind, at any
rate, Böker 2305. Berecyntias was a wind blowing at
Miletus from the mountain range Berecyntus in Phrygia,
thus a northeast wind. The name transferred to Sinope

in Pontus, when a colony was founded there, Böker 2291.
Thus, names of winds are generalized through the movements of traders and sailors, through movements of peo-
ples, and from confusion of terms.

# INDICES

# INDEX OF TERMS AND TOPICS

(Numbers refer to Sections)